Praise for *The Circle*

"This stunning anthology will not only appeal to those familiar with Brussels incognito, but also to those with an appreciation for divine inspiration, as international writers engage with a capital city and its unique way of life."

—*Brussels Express*

"This collection of short stories, poems, fairy tales and film scripts is proof of Brussels's international talent. Entertaining takes on life, love and revenge are complemented by nuanced thoughts about everything that makes us human…. The collection of literature dives into topics like religion, minorities, grief and terrorism and does so in a respectful and reflective manner. Its unusual mix of topics and forms reveals a usually hidden face of Brussels."

—*Midwest Book Review*

"Over fifty contributions contain some real gems. Short film scripts, non-fiction pieces, fairy tales and poems are united in their unique portrayal of the surreal aspect of Brussels exploring different dimensions of the human condition.... While generous with light and humorous everyday topics, *The Circle* also respectfully takes on complicated and controversial issues like terrorism, race, religion, diversity and grief...."

—*Pleiades Book Review*

"The Anthology is made up of fifty-five contributions by thirty-four authors (including award-winning Jeanie Keogh and Colin Walsh) from nineteen countries. It dabbles in poetry, prose and script; fiction and non-fiction, packing in a number of themes: fantasy, love, death, violence, humiliation, humour, devotion, grief, loss, history, memory.... The Anthology has something for everyone, and it is a tribute to this great city to read the beauty of English embraced by many nationalities and cultures."

—*Together Magazine*

THE CIRCLE

A Brussels Anthology

Edited by Patrick ten Brink

Harvard Square Editions

2018

The Circle

Cover design: J Caleb Clark ©

ISBN: 978-1-941861-70-7

Published by
Harvard Square Editions
www.harvardsquareeditions.org

.

Table of Contents

Introduction

WELCOME TO *THE CIRCLE*. This anthology contains fifty-five contributions by thirty-four authors from nineteen countries—anchored in multicultural Brussels.

Andreas Bergsten kicks off the anthology with a bitingly funny piece, 'Poetic License, by Gilbert Jones', written just after the Brexit vote. Jeanie Keogh nails loss in 'If at First You Don't Succeed' as does Joost Hiltermann in 'KAWA's Calvary', which courageously touches upon a people's grief—that of the Kurds who suffered genocidal actions—a story that needs to be told and learned from. Read the chapter, and when it is out, get the book. You will never think of popcorn scooping the same way after you read Colin Walsh's prizewinning 'The Flare Carves Itself Through the Dark'. It might also change your view of life.

Dimitris Politis' 'The Ordinary Colours of an Extraordinary Day' captures the sights and sounds of a traveller's fateful metro journey when a bomb exploded. Mimi Kunz offers a humourous yet melancholic imagining of Brussels in the future, digging back to the present in 'The Museum of Favourite Things'. Richard Boland's 'Above and Beyond All Reason' is a beautiful and deeply moving tribute to friends lost to AIDS and to the love of friends who helped in troubling times. These are just a few of the little jewels you will find in this anthology.

To whet your appetite further, C.S. Begu's poem 'To the City of Hopes and Steel' presents the challenges facing migrants, using dark humour to explore the controversial theme of immigration. We have two disturbingly funny stories of brother-and-sister relationships: Kevin Dwyer's 'Little Piggy Come to Play' and Aisling Henrard's 'Lining their Pockets'. Genevieve Shapiro's 'Santa's Bell' shows that love can cross zombie-human prejudice barriers, and Klavs Skovsholm tells a touching tale in 'Belle of the Ball'. T.D. Arkenberg' 'Aftershock' courageously tackles race, religion, the prejudice and terrorism that has defaced the Brussels we love.

Voilà, a glimpse into the pieces in *The Circle*. I hope you enjoy them all. I have.

—Patrick ten Brink, Editor, *The Circle*

Andreas Bergsten

'Poetic License, by Gilbert Jones'

*This is entirely a work of fiction,
and will hopefully so remain.*

I WAS SCHEDULED to read my poems to a live audience at
seven p.m. Since I was going to leave town later that
night, I had a lot to take care of. I kept pushing one
item down my to-do list until it was the only one left. I
inhaled deeply and phoned my father in London. I told
him I was hoping to stay in the cottage for a while. He
never uses it in the winter, so he said okay, for £500 a
month.

"Having some of my tax money back from Brussels,"
he said. "Why come home? Did you get fired?"

"I work for the European Commission, Dad. They're
stuck with me."

"No one's indispensable, son."

"But some are unextractable. I'm like a parasite
lodged in the central nervous system. The Commission
would have to blow its brains out to get rid of me."

"A parasite inside a parasite—and you whined about

me voting for Brexit?"

He would have loved to have that discussion again, but I wasn't giving him the pleasure.

"I'm taking some time off to finish my novel," I said. "They're as happy to have me on leave as in the office."

"Your novel. Another service to mankind. What's wrong with people? All and sundry vomiting books. You're almost 40, Gilbert. Isn't it time you did something I could tell my neighbours about without blushing? Maybe create some real people?"

Once, I had sent him a story of mine, about an old grouch poisoning his son's life. I had hoped he would be mortified, maybe even remorseful.

"It was readable, I suppose," he had said. "I'm certainly glad you can appreciate the travails of parenthood. How that poor old man is never rid of his weakling son."

I was stumped.

"You actually liked it?"

"I wouldn't go that far. I can't say I learned anything new or felt anything special."

"Those were never your talents, Dad."

After that, I didn't send him anything, never talked about my writing.

I agreed to pay two months' rent in advance plus a £500 deposit, in case I broke anything. Then, I hung up, before he had a chance to continue his list of complaints against me.

So, this was it. I was leaving Brussels, hopefully never to return. Twelve dull years of pointless work, fickle friends, and fries with mayo. I had managed to save a decent amount of money, though, and to hone my fiction writing skills. Now, it was time for me to come into my own, to shed the bland civil-servant persona I had adopted, to burst into the open with all my talents on display. I had decided to start this new phase of my life with thunder and lightning, and this night afforded me the perfect opportunity. Yes, my voice would carry, finally. Scores would be settled.

The Literati bookshop looked so stereotypically cosy in the drizzly night that I had to laugh. The staff had dimmed the electric lights and put lanterns with real candles on the tables showcasing new titles. Normally closing at 7 p.m., they were happy to house our event after hours. A perfect match: the creatively struggling writers' group launching its self-published anthology in the financially struggling English bookshop. Mutual Commiseration Night. The counter next to the entrance was stacked with lukewarm bag-in-box wine, crates of strong beer (this being Belgium), and trays with bone-dry crackers sporting bland Cheddar (the group being mostly English). A sizeable crowd for the smallish shop, maybe sixty heads, all family and friends cajoled into coming, all concentrating on the free drinks.

I accessed the 'Poetry gallery' from a freakish art nouveau spiral staircase in the overwrought-iron style the Belgians are so proud of. I was up there with Jessica and Sven, on the narrow balcony lining the wall to the right of the entrance. The shop area was cluttered, but the ceiling height was at least 18 feet. The narrow gangway was perfect for the performance we were about to deliver; the three of us reading from the anthology, swaying above the main floor where the guests sloshed their drinks on the worn parquet.

The gallery was also well suited for my own purposes, since it had a little back door on the other end from the iron staircase, opening onto a regular flight of stairs that led to a back entrance. I checked that it was clear to exit, and placed my coat and bag on the steps.

I persuaded Sven to let me go first.

"Better have the more accomplished pieces linger in peoples' minds towards the end," I fawned. "We'll let Jessica go second, with her cat story, and save you for the finale."

He was going to read out a dense page of verse called 'Iterationes', a Post Traumatic Stress Disorder poem for Brussels after the terrorist attacks, he claimed, playing reverently on the flashbacks that surviving victims were suffering from. He said it was necessary for the audience to read along, so he wanted to print out his poem and distribute it before his reading. That way there could be an interesting discussion afterwards.

I guessed everyone would be happy to forget his

poem straight away but didn't say so. Instead, I had got him hooked on the idea of projecting the poem high up on the white wall to our right, with the portable projector I had nicked from work. I set it up and placed Sven's laptop on a three-legged stool between us, my own memory stick plugged in with a few slides for my presentation.

I cleared my throat to get people's attention, but I prolonged my hemming and hawing and segued into a roaring cough as if about to heave up my intestines. They all went silent all right and looked up at us with alarm. Sven turned to me and put his hand on my shoulder, probably prepared to perform the Heimlich manoeuvre. I winked at him, and his mouth fell open. He didn't think I had it in me—not meek and formal Gilbert. I smiled at him, triumphantly, I hope, as if to say: Guess again, stupid. It's showtime!

No one is convinced by unsolicited denials. That is why disclaimers always sound dubious—cases of protesting too much. I know the purpose is to avoid libel suits, but it is still disfiguring. An ugly stain on the marble face of art. Unless you make the stain an integral part of the art.

I wonder where I stand now vis-à-vis libel laws. I willfully went overboard and prefaced my reciting with no less than three evasive actions. The first one was an intentionally lame joke just to embarrass the culture-snobs, especially Sven.

"No animals were harmed in the making of this poem," I declared in a stentorian voice. Which was a lie. I came up with that one swatting a fly at my writing desk. The provocation worked. Sven winced and flipped through the pages of the anthology to see if this was really in the book. Of course, it wasn't.

Next, I delivered the standard dodge, but with a twist.

"Any resemblance to actual persons or events, past or present, is pure, dumb luck." Which was another lie, since I was quite intentionally about to name names of real and very present persons. The falsehoods in my first two fudges gave me the idea for a third.

"These disclaimers are all part of the work of art, and hence subject to poetic license." Self-disclaiming disclaimers. I figured that would leave everyone properly befuddled, while primed to believe I was about to reveal some outrageous truth.

"Knock it off," Sven hissed in my ear. "Just read your goddamn haikai!"

"Forget it," I whispered back. "There will be no haikus." Sven's jaw dropped again.

I hate my haikus (plural: haiku, not haikai, but who cares)—I hate all haikus. Toddler poetry, impossible to fail at, exceedingly hard to make interesting. I just scribbled a couple of them down for the anthology, to seem like a good sport. Robotically counting syllables, according to received idiocy—the corresponding metric in English ought to be stresses. I was never going to waste my serious writing in this company. I even contemplated using a pen name, but that would irreparably have pissed off the others. I wanted to save that effect for something grander. Counting words, my three disclaimers beat the actual "poem" by 40 words to 33. Another inanity to take delight in, though no one would be counting words by the time I had finished.

I pressed the arrow key on Sven's laptop, and the first line quivered darkly on the lit-up wall.

"**There was a poor sod name of Cory**," I boomed.

This was more of an assessment than a fact, but the one true sentiment in my limerick. If anyone in our group qualified as a poor sod, Cory did. There are a dozen or so of us, all English speakers stranded in Brussels, all aspiring writers, meeting every Wednesday night in the back room of Huis van Dirk, a grimy Flemish pub downtown. We read each other our pieces, give each other feedback, and have ourselves a drink. Some usually stay on after the sessions, having themselves several more drinks.

I get along with everyone. I don't particularly like anyone, but I mostly keep quiet or mumble non-committal phrases. None of them gets my writing, so their feedback is practically useless to me. They insist on calling my book science fiction, which it is not, and either they are into Scifi and want me to change everything according to some beaten-to-death formula, or they are not into Scifi and couldn't care less. It is going to be such a satisfying moment when my novel is picked up by a major publishing house. I've just got the one rewrite left. And it is speculative fiction, thank you, of the more intellectual kind. That's why it doesn't matter exactly how the technology works on Jupiter in the year 2,222, or why I don't get into the genetics of human-alien miscegenation. Who cares? It is an existential rumination, dressed up in space opera garb. But no one here seems to get that. The professional critics will, though.

Anyway, the poor-soddiness of Cory: He is a morose and brooding guy, who drinks way too much, and never finishes things. Let me admit that he is unusual, especially for our group, since he is a really good writer. I would never say it to his face, but I do admire his work. He gets a lot of encouragement from the group, everyone always imploring him to submit his stories to an agent or enter them in contests. He smiles wistfully at the praise but never gets around to quite finishing his texts. And then, he's got this Irish temper. I've seen him snap and get into arguments with strangers on several occasions, especially when drinking hard after sessions. He even started a fistfight once, when some poor Walloon honestly mistook him for an Englishman. And I think his marriage is miserable; there has been a lot of gossip about that— though they gossip about everything. His stories are deeply misogynistic, but he never gets called out on it, because his self-loathing colours his male characters just as detestable. I once heard him drunkenly complain about faithless women to the bartender, Jaap, who doesn't speak much English, but who nodded sympathetically and kept the beer flowing.

I have never cared for Cory. His feedback is always terse, often damaging, and he has never had a kind word to say about my writing. Sometimes he just shrugs and says, "Pass," after my reading, clearly communicating that he finds my work unworthy of his attention. So, I don't regret a thing; he had it coming.

I pressed the arrow key again, and a picture of Cory appeared on the wall, something I copied from the writers' group's web page. He looked sullen and dishevelled, as always, copper hair hanging down over his pale eyes, a beefy hand stretched out towards the camera as if to avert it. When I spotted Cory in the crowd below, staring at his picture, I quickly flipped to the next slide, with the limerick again, a second line added:

There was a poor sod name of Cory
"whose wife went the way of his story," I bellowed.

This was partly a reference to a true event. Cory had lost a story. A few months ago, he showed up at a meeting with just four copies of a short story—we usually bring a dozen, so everyone can read along and annotate. Cory told us his computer had broken down in the middle of printing, and since he hadn't made any back-ups, these were the only copies. The story, called 'It's me', was a beautiful and sad post-mortem of a marriage. For once, his female character didn't come off as a manipulative bitch. Even the male narrator seemed gracious and sad. The piece was a cross between a lament and a tribute. The group entreated him to type it up again on another computer and send it off to some magazines. This time, he said he would actually do just that. And maybe he would have, who knows, if I hadn't nicked all four copies from his bag when he went to the gents later that night. I didn't stay around to see how he reacted, but the next Wednesday, when he told the group, I realised he didn't suspect me. The group was dismayed and encouraged him to write it down from memory, but Cory had regained his gloomy passivity and repeated that it wasn't meant to be.

Nevertheless, my limerick line was opaque, and I didn't expect anyone to figure out why I was mentioning Cory's wife. Those who knew Elena looked over at her, where she stood towards the back of the crowd, leaning against a bookcase. Her black hair was set in a loose knot, her dark eyes searching out the screen of her cell phone, oblivious to my reading and the slight commotion it caused. I hit the arrow key and presented the third line:

There was a poor sod name of Cory
Whose wife went the way of his story
"Both were stolen by Sven,"

I hollered, letting my voice enter an accusing falsetto.

Here I departed into true fiction. I may dislike Cory, but Sven I truly hate. He is one of the few non-native English speakers in the group. He's Swedish, or Finnish, maybe—I keep forgetting, a blonde, long-legged goof. He's always preening, joking, and flirting. Acting as if everyone found him suave and charismatic. Aren't Scandinavians supposed to be unsociable and reserved? His writing is rubbish. Overly brainy poetry he makes so complicated so no one can figure out he is not a genius. Except me. I see right through him. I think he comes around just to get attention, have some drinks—and an excuse to call himself a writer. He uses off-putting literary phrases even when he speaks, which he does constantly. After a few beers his tongue grows unwieldy, and he starts sounding like the Swedish chef in the Muppet show.

I had him down as a shallow poseur from the start, but what made me decide to do something about him was the feedback he had given me a couple of months ago. I was reading out the part of my novel where the protagonist makes love to this girl he's met (well, a female, kind of, at least—she is an alien). It is always a balancing act, writing convincingly about sex, but I had finally managed to pull it off. Daring, but not vulgar; heartfelt, but not mawkish. And I could avoid being trite or embarrassing when extolling body parts and describing the technical aspects since I could make half of the anatomy up.

Sven had guffawed all the way through my reading. Didn't even try to hide it. And he could hardly wait to comment.

"The most brilliant text you've ever read out to us," he said. But then he went on to call it a hilarious caricature of a perverted psyche, the obsessive ramblings of someone who had never had sex. He is a medical doctor, the lowliest kind—a psychiatrist, but not practicing. He serves on some EU board to improve mental health in Europe. He could start by leaving the continent. As a communications officer, I eat off the EU table myself, but at least I don't pretend there's any point to what I do. Sven holds forth on mental health stakeholders (who isn't one?), policy initiatives, and the importance of increased health for economic growth—hardly lifted from the Hippocratic oath.

Doctor or not, you just don't say things like that when you give feedback. I smiled and played along, acting as if the passage was indeed meant as a joke, not to give him the satisfaction. But I decided this was one stunt he wouldn't pull unpunished.

Now, Sven stared at his name projected on the wall and called out to me.

"Gilbert, what the hell is this?"

I answered him by pressing the key for the concluding two lines—time was of the essence, and kept my voice thunderous over the buzz rising up from the audience:

There was a poor sod name of Cory
whose wife went the way of his story.
Both were stolen by Sven,
"one was fucked, one was then
put online to Sven's undeserved glory."

I immediately switched to the last slide. The complete limerick was at the top, condensed, but clearly readable. Below, the slide was vertically divided, showing two images, side by side.

On the left, a photograph showing Sven and Cory's wife sitting at a restaurant table drinking wine. Their heads were close, as in furtive intimacy. Elena's right arm was resting on the table. Sven was turned towards her, his hand on her arm, and her left hand was squeezing his.

I knew that Cory had never seen the picture or heard about the encounter. Sven was always sucking up to Cory—the only one he treated as an equal, and I knew they socialised outside the group. Last month, Sven had phoned me and asked if I would meet him and Elena in a brasserie tucked away somewhere in Ixelles, far from Cory's usual hangouts in the city. They were planning a surprise party for Cory's 45th birthday and wanted me to compile a photo tribute. Sven knows about 'Brussels Unawares', my somewhat popular photoblog, and he has never hesitated to bother me with requests for help in computer matters before. This time, I was happy to oblige.

When I reached the meeting place, I parked across the street. Luckily, I spotted Sven and Elena at an outside table and texted him that I would be a little late. I sat in my car for fifteen minutes and took well over a hundred photos of them. Nothing I saw indicated any indiscretion, but since Sven is always flirty with women, leaning in, touching them, it was a great photo-op. The picture I eventually settled on is thoroughly disingenuous. Elena was in fact about to remove Sven's hand from her arm, but that is not what the picture suggests.

The lower right part of the slide was a screen dump from the Australian online magazine 'Up from Down Under', where I had managed to place the story I had stolen from Cory. I could have created a fake website, but I wanted it to remain unclear what was true and what was fictitious. So I submitted the story to several small, but serious, outlets. The Australians jumped at the piece, and I had to stall them a bit, not to have it published prematurely. The screen-dump clearly showed the magazine header, the title, 'It's me', followed by the author byline, 'by Sven Lundberg'. The first lines of the text were visible, and, for those who remembered the piece, undeniably the start of Cory's stolen story.

After I had finished reading my limerick, everyone stared at the wall with the images of Sven, Cory's wife, and the hijacked short story. Complete silence descended. Then, a snarling sound was heard from below, and Cory came pounding up the staircase. Sven didn't move a limb, didn't utter a sound. No smart retorts. I snatched my memory stick from his laptop and moved away, to the other side of Jessica, who stood silent and inert.

When Cory climbed onto the gallery, I retreated to the back door, one hand on the handle. But he didn't come for me; he went for Sven. Everything was strangely silent and still, except for the weird rumbling sound from Cory's throat. I glimpsed the audience below as a sea of beige ovals with dark splotches, upturned faces with gaping mouths. Sven had turned towards his attacker, arms outstretched as if expecting a hug, but Cory just swung at him, mid-step, hitting him in the face. Sven twirled and grabbed the railing, leaning over it, a dollop of blood splashing down onto the New Young Adult fiction table. Cory seized him by the legs and hoisted him over the railing with such force, the stupid Scandinavian sailed a good five feet out from the balcony, crashing head first into a smaller table stacked with glasses of white wine. When he rolled over on the floor, his face was studded with pieces of broken glass, and blood trickled prettily.

Sound and motion erupted everywhere. Sven was twisting and whining. People were screaming, rushing up to him, shouting to each other to call for an ambulance, call the police. Only Cory was still, staring down at the chaos below. I wanted to stay and savour it all, but I didn't dare. Instead, I slipped through the back door, picked up my coat and bag on the stairs, tumbled outside and ran the three blocks to where my rental was parked.

I just sat in the car for a while, panting. It was such a rush—I still shiver thinking about it. I felt godlike, Godlike—my words instantiated. Gilbert said: Let there be mayhem! And there was fucking mayhem. And Gilbert saw that it was good. Sorry for the blasphemy, and the cursing, but this happens to be what it feels like to be a truly successful writer, when the impact of your words is indisputable. Instant feedback, not filtered through some arrogant know-it-all amateur critic's brain, but by the very rearrangement of the material world around you. Feels bloody awesome. Just thought you literary types would like to know.

*

Andreas Bergsten is a Swedish psychologist who started writing seriously in English under the auspices of the Brussels Writers Circle during his four-year stay in Belgium. Last summer, he returned to Stockholm for an inverted sabbatical year of work in consulting psychology. In the autumn of 2018, he will relocate to Beijing to rewrite his debut novel, The Rift.

Jeanie Keogh

If at First You Don't Succeed

BILL LISTENED TO THE MELODY of an ice cream truck sing-songing past and was nostalgic. Against all odds, ice cream trucks had passed the test of time where other things—film photography, full service gas stations, his only son—had not.

"Bill, you're dawdling."

"Am I?"

Bill looked at his wife Nancy standing on the pavement in front of the door that led to yet another memorial service for their son. Her face was a perfectly-iced cake: fragile and hard.

Bill had had his fill of public mourning—first the wake, then the funeral—but Nancy had said she'd feel badly if they didn't attend. She was often saying she felt badly, when she passed road kill, when reading the newspaper, when turning down a golf invitation.

He adjusted the knot of his tie and put his hand on her back to escort her inside.

The room was a sort of studio with sagging wooden floors, high ceilings and dust-caked skylights. Tibetan flags hung from the exposed beams, and the air smelled faintly of body odour and musky perfume. Everyone was barefooted. A few shirtless men were giving massages. Two women with colourful dreadlocks wearing what looked like elfin cloaks were practising yoga. Beside them a woman hoola hooped, her hoop swinging over the heads of a group of people cuddling on the floor on mismatching throw pillows. Opposite them, a man with several tattoos was leading a call-and-response meditation in a different language. Bill's heart seized. At the end of the room there was a large photograph of David, sticks of incense burning in front of it, creating a smoke screen in front of his smiling face.

"What the hell is this?" Bill whispered to his wife.

"It's some sort of ritual," Nancy hissed through bared teeth.

"It's a bloody New Age circus!"

"Shhh!"

So these were the people he had to thank for teaching David to give up striving toward a career, instead embracing a life of ride sharing, dumpster diving, and communal living. Ageing trust fund kids, the lot of them.

Bill and Nancy took off their shoes. A man wearing a Native American headdress greeted them with a ceremonious bow and then waved pungent smoke from a smouldering bunch of plants in Bill's face with the wing of a dead bird. Bill lowered his head so the smoke wouldn't get in his eyes and stared at the man's cracked feet and curling, yellowed toenails.

"Welcome, Wise Ones, to the Spirit Flight. My name is Brother Eagle. Please find your way to one of the stations, whichever one calls to you," the man said before moving off to suffocate someone else.

Bill was incredulous. The man was White!

"I thought we were coming to a memorial service, not a spiritual retreat," he said under his breath.

Nancy looked at Bill in the way that induced near panic attacks in him since he met her 40 years ago. He had mistaken this look for love when they were first dating, but later realized it was intense expectation.

Bill led her to an empty spot by the wall between a big drum and a statue of Buddha.

"Do you recognize anyone?" Nancy asked.

Bill watched a man in tribal-looking body paint perform an interpretive dance. Dust particles stirred up by the man's feet caught the light of sunset and hovered in a slow-moving helix. Bill felt Nancy elbow him. It took him a minute to remember what she had asked.

"Not a soul," Bill answered, before she could ask again.

All of these people had been with David on the beach at the island music festival when he died. The thought made Bill break out in a sweat. There had been over a thousand people there and not one of them had noticed David had gone missing.

The man called Brother Eagle began to make guttural sounds and stamp his feet to get people's attention. When everyone in the room had stood in attention, Brother Eagle lifted up the skull of a horned animal from his prop table. People gathered in a circle and the room went silent.

"We begin the ceremony to honour our Brother David on his sacred journey from the Earthly realm to the Fifth Plane."

Bill glanced furtively at the rapt faces.

Brother Eagle carried the horned skull over to David's photograph and placed it on the floor by the incense. He then picked up a drum and beat it three times in the direction of each corner of the room.

"David, you have been summoned by the Great Spirits in Father Sky. We call you forth to help us understand the divine message in your passing over into the beyond."

Bill clenched his hands into fists. This esoteric buffoonery was no way to honour his son's life. He had agreed to come to a memorial service, not a sorcery workshop led by a half-cocked voodoo charlatan with a penchant for cultural appropriation. He glanced quickly at Nancy and watched the muscles of her jaw tighten as she swallowed. He had become very familiar with that skeletal hinge in front of her ear. He'd watched it at the psychiatrist's office ten years ago after David's first of many suicide attempts, following a poor performance review of his amateur theatre troupe. Bill remembered going into his son's hospital room and finding David asleep. Bill had tucked David's bandaged wrists gently under the hospital blanket, so that Nancy would not have to see them, and balled up his bloodied unicorn costume. Standing in the hall outside the psychiatrist's office afterward, Nancy told the doctor their son went through ups and downs, but was most certainly not manic depressive. Then she broke down. Bill muffled the disturbing sound with his chest, until she'd lost her voice.

Although the family went through the charade of recovery, Bill secretly feared it was only a matter of time before a bad combination of recreational drugs and a change in David's medication resulted in a successful attempt.

Brother Eagle closed his eyes and began shaking a rattle, breathing in short bursts of air. He shuffled in a small circle, the stone pendants around his neck chiming against one another.

"I am cleansing this space so that your enlightened soul can return from the place it has wandered on to, before making a final departure," he said.

Bill looked at his watch: 8:32 p.m. The clock on the wall read 8:35. It made him slightly, but not unmanageably, anxious that his watch was slower by three minutes. He reset it to 8:36 and put it back on his wrist, noticing his watch tan from his Bermuda holiday with Nancy. The holiday had been cut short by a phone call from police at 8:35 a.m. to tell them the news.

On a beach on Texada Island, in the dead of night, David had walked out into the ocean and ended his life. As Nancy packed their bags to return to Canada, Bill installed himself at the swim-up bar and drank until he no longer pictured David leaving the still-warm sand, the water lapping against David's knees, his armpits, into his mouth.

Bill's thoughts returned to the room. "We will now begin the ceremony of David's Crossing Over, saying a prayer for his journey on to the higher plane," the Brother Eagle said, "I invite you to say a silent blessing, or voice your heart, as the Spirit moves you." Bill ran his tongue between his teeth, fantasizing about how hard he would bite Brother Eagle *if the Spirit moved him*.

Brother Eagle, aided by the shirtless men, carried a large stone cauldron filled with water and placed it in the centre of the circle. Then they handed out tea lights to everyone. Brother Eagle blessed the cauldron and then lit a large candle in front of it, instructing people to come forward one by one, light their tea lights, and place them on the floor around the cauldron.

One of the yoga women entered into the circle, lit her candle, and began to cry.

"David, I know you wouldn't have wanted us to be sad. I know you didn't do it out of despair, but because you belong to a higher order. Bless you, dear friend," she said, placing her candle on the floor.

Bill was enraged that this woman, who Bill had never met or heard tale of, had the gall to claim she knew what David would or wouldn't want.

The interpretive dancer went next.

"David, there are such things as people who are too good for this world, and your death will always be a painful, ever-present reminder of this. I will miss you, brother," he said.

These people were hypocrites; in all the time Bill had spent with David, David's phone had only rung once. It was a telemarketer.

Nancy emitted a balloon-like squeak as her face crumpled. She hid her face in Bill's shoulder.

"Why?" she asked.

Bill did not know how to answer this, whether she was asking, *Why did our son have a mental illness? What did we do wrong?* or even *Why did I marry you?*, but her asking it unravelled a memory.

David had just been discharged from the hospital after an overdose. Nancy thought it would be good for him to go to the cottage. Instead, for four days, David did nothing but wander back and forth along the stretch of oceanfront. Bill joined him, pretending to comb the beach for shells. Half-an-hour in, Bill broke the silence with, "Look David, a shark's tooth!" which fell flat. Bill was not gifted at starting conversations. He searched for something positive to say. The only thing that came to him were the morale-boosting quotes he wrote on white boards at company meetings, and he knew damn well this would not work on his son.

Nancy squeezed Bill's arm, bringing him back to the present. He looked down at the nails digging into his forearm and his eyes rested on her wedding ring, which had grown tight on her finger over the years. She'd complained about it when she was pregnant, her hands and feet swelling along with her belly, but brushed aside his suggestion to have it resized, confident it would fit her after she delivered.

Nancy elbowed him in the ribs. Thinking she wanted to be comforted, Bill put his arm around her waist, but felt her stiffen.

"It's your turn," Nancy hissed.

Bill realized he was the last one to place his candle in the circle. He took a few steps in, put down his unlit candle, and stepped back to his place beside his wife. Bill was smugly satisfied that his candle was far away from the others; closer, in fact, to the edge of the circle than the middle.

Brother Eagle announced: "We will now begin the ceremony to worship David's tribe."

He approached Bill and Nancy.

"These are the Great Elders of our Cherished Tribesman, David Fletcher. As the people who gave him life, we collectively honour you."

A few people raised their hands to their hearts and foreheads in prayer. Others held their hands outstretched or over their heads.

Nancy's nostrils were flaring, an early warning sign

that she was going to break down again. Bill cleared his throat loudly in defiance, but before he could protest, Brother Eagle guided him and Nancy into the circle and submerged their hands in the cauldron of water.

Looking at his hands under the water and seeing the small bubbles forming around the hair follicles on his skin reminded Bill of the only father-son tradition he and David shared: taking the first swim of each summer together at the cottage. They would run off the dock and dive into the cold water, willing themselves not to break the surface until their lungs convulsed. The last one up was the winner.

Bill steeled himself, fearing he would snap: his son had drowned himself and this idiotic demagogue was making them put their hands in water as if it would heal them. He was making a mockery of everything he and Nancy had done to prevent David from funnelling down the rabbit hole of self-loathing.

Brother Eagle put his hands on the crown of Bill's head. "William Fletcher, we thank you for bringing David into this world, and honour your role in making him who he was."

Bill felt a burning sensation in his chest and his eyes became hot. The last time he cried was on a streetcar in Toronto when he was ten. He couldn't remember why. He fought to get a hold of himself, breathing slowly and deeply as he remembered Nancy doing years ago in Lamaze classes.

David's birth.

Bill was only partly aware of what Brother Eagle said next. He felt as if the wind had been knocked out of him as he realized he had utterly failed his son. The piano lessons, private school, prestigious acting academy, ski holidays—a waste. He'd not hugged David enough, given him enough encouragement. He'd been too critical. Regret ripped through Bill's body and his heart snagged thinking of all the things they had never done together.

Bill gasped for air as the sobs racked his body like a violent cough. The grief thundered out of him and he thrashed and cried out in an animal-like howl. His wife drew in a sharp breath. Through watery eyes he could still make out the stricken faces of the crowd as they shrank back against the wall in fear. Some of them were leaving the room. But Bill had no anger left, only a hollow well inside him that he could yell I LOVE YOU, DAVID down as loud as he could and hear only a desperate, lonely echo.

Exhausted, Bill let Brother Eagle lower him to the floor. Lying on his back, Bill thought of his son lying in the water like flotsam, belly up to the sky. Tears dripped down Bill's face and pooled in his ears.

Nancy's face appeared over his from upside down.

He watched her mouth form words, the top lip moving, the bottom one staying in place. She looked like a fish. Bill remembered that if you look at something from upside down long enough, the brain rights the image.

What he couldn't remember was how the mind knows which way is up.

*

Jeanie Keogh's stories have been published in the Canadian literary magazines Riddle Fence, Grain, FreeFall, The Puritan, and Matrix. Her story 'The Offbeat' won second prize in Broken Pencil's 2013 Deathmatch contest. Her one-act play Baby Making was produced at the Harbourfront Centre in Toronto, Canada by Summerworks Theatre Festival and staged at The Geordie Theatre in Montreal. The story in this collection, 'If At First You Don't Succeed', was previously shortlisted for the Vancouver Writers Festival contest.

Colin Walsh

The Flare Carves Itself Through The Dark

'The Flare Carves Itself Through The Dark' won the RTE Radio 1 Francis MacManus Short Story Competition and is reprinted here with kind permission of RTE.

ABSOLUTE MELTER of a summer that year. The air throbbed, everything solid dilating. Shirtless lads with see-sawing shoulders glowered with 99s dribbling over their knuckles while the young wans glistened in the shade, make-up warping in the heat. Even the tarmac was sweating. I spent my breaks on the warm steps of the Cineplex, watching them suck the last nectar out of the hottest August the town ever had.

I'd been inside the Cineplex since the Leaving, shovelling the popcorn, pouring the popcorn, serving the popcorn. Midges swarmed in drifts around my bike every afternoon as I cycled to work along the water's edge. Even when the whole town slurred, the river flowed on and on. The evening sunsets there were nightmares of tortured colour. I cycled home at their tail-end after work, headphones in, my bike gliding beneath strange veins of light which coursed over the town till darkness fell.

That Saturday, the final one of the holidays, was the summer's nuclear peak; one final flare and it'd gutter out like a candle. Everything felt haunted by the future. After that weekend, a fresh batch of kids would bust the town walls open and barrel down arterial roads that had once looped off the world. They'd spill giddy onto motorways and get bellied off to bigger lives at colleges up and down the country. I'd be one of them; successfully lost to the future, not looking back. I'd just turned eighteen and spent the past year getting up at 5 a.m. to do two hour's study before breakfast, feathering my bedroom walls with flashcards till it looked like the lair of some maniac. Now college beckoned. I was about to get myself born.

The Cineplex foyer was a riot of chatter for the final Saturday showing. I was working my last shift alone, which I actually enjoyed: I shovelled the popcorn, poured the popcorn, served the popcorn; I took the tickets, tore the tickets, returned the tickets. The foyer quivered like a coiled spring, people ordering their sweets in rabid voices, jabbering loudly about their college plans. They never asked about my plans, though we'd all been in school together. That was okay. I'd decided long ago that our town was a nowhere; it was okay to be a nothing in a nowhere. Next week I'd finally be somewhere; I might become a something in a somewhere.

In the queue I saw Teabag Lyons and his girlfriend, Lisa. A curd of gum hopped about Lisa's mouth like a swab of popcorn bouncing around a pot. Teabag had one hand tucked into her arse pocket and the other down the front of his trackies. He eyeballed the world, daring it to have an opinion. At the time, I had no strong emotions for Teabag, only the vague muscle-memory sort-of-fear everyone had of him and his brother. His brother had emigrated to Australia but got turned back at the border. People called him Boomerang behind his back. I didn't even know his real name.

Lisa grinned when they reached the counter. 'Howya Dan!'

I blushed a hello. We'd been in playschool together. Now she was grinding her jaw, making her order, eyes all moon-pooled. We used to share crayons.

Teabag didn't even look at me. Something was off about his face, his mouth.

'Off to college next week?' Lisa said, not waiting for an answer. 'You were always such a brain-box. Where you heading?'

'Dublin,' I said. 'Trinity.'

'Well, law-dee-daw!' Her cheeks shimmered. 'Your grandparents must be thrilled.'

I smiled, despite the rash coiling up my neck, because Nanny and Grandad had both cried happy tears when I told them. Grandad hid his by putting on the kettle. 'Trinity College', he repeated all evening, in accents of increasingly absurd poshness. *'Treh-no-taaaay-caw-laaaaaaaaage.'*

I put their Cokes on the counter and began telling her about my plans when Teabag cut me off, clicking his fingers in my face. I saw for the first time that he was wearing a blue mouthguard over his teeth. 'Nyust gib us the muckin' bobcorn,' he said. I bowed my head and served the popcorn.

'Tell your Nanny I was asking after her,' Lisa said as they left.

Teabag shouldered into Eoin Duggan, nearly drowning him with two Cokes. Before they disappeared into Screen 4, Lisa called back, 'Enjoy Dublin!'

Duggan came to the counter, rubbing his chest where Teabag had rammed him. 'Nobody's gonna miss that mong-child', he said.

'What happened his mouth?' I said.

'Himself and Boomerang pissed off the wrong people,' he said. 'Some lads got a hold of Teabag last week to prove the point. Made him bite on a brick while they kicked his belly asunder. He has to wear that blue yoke till he gets surgery.'

'Jesus Christ,' I said.

'Giveths and taketh away,' Duggan grinned, making an exaggerated sign of the cross. I clocked the '18 Today' birthday badge attached to his Slipknot T-shirt.

'Happy birthday,' I said.

'Cheers dude', he laughed. 'Myself and Rachel are

meeting a crew in the woods after the film if you fancy.'

'Yeah, maybe,' I lied. Duggan and I used to share Pokémon cards when we were kids. He had never once picked on me.

'Give us your number so,' he said. 'We'll keep a few cans aside for you.'

I didn't want to go bushing in the woods, but I gave him my number anyway.

Duggan's girlfriend Rachel called from the door of Screen 4.

'Come on,' she said, 'I don't wanna miss the trailers.'

When they left, the foyer was empty, and I was alone.

During the film I hoovered the empty auditoriums, counted the till and imagined my final bike ride home. Just me and the gargling water. I'd stop for a moment to watch the river one last time. That's how I'd say goodbye to the town. No tears or big gesture, just some intimate salutation to the turbulence twisting past me before life began. Then Dublin. Housemates. Friends. Maybe a girlfriend, one day. All those names from TV and radio: 'the Luas'; 'the DART'; 'Stephen's Green'; 'the Grand Canal'. The neon lights of a real city in rain.

I was thinking all this when the door of Screen 4 burst open and Duggan ran across the foyer. His hair and t-shirt were drenched in Coke, the birthday badge gone. Rachel came calling after him, but Duggan was already out the door.

She stormed up to me, glaring daggers. 'Aren't you supposed to be keeping an eye on things here?' she snarled. Mascara was worming down her cheeks. She pointed to Screen 4. 'That gummy prick in there is ruining *everything*.'

There was no manager. There was only me. I said I'd take care of it.

I watched myself cross the foyer, enter the darkness of Screen 4; I heard the click of my torch, and saw the lightbeam splitting the dark. I felt the room turn, the ripple of anticipation. Teabag was sitting with his feet on the backs of two empty seats. Lisa was feasting on his neck. I saw the way he watched me approaching. I still see it.

I cleared my throat, not sure what to say. But he spoke first.

'Whannya thmilin' bout?' he said.

There was a long pause.

Then I said, 'I'm not smiling.' I could hear the tremor in my voice.

'So you're gibbin' me cheek?' he said.

'He's not giving cheek, babe,' Lisa said. Teabag stood slowly, his eyes never leaving me. Lisa reached for his sleeve, but he slapped her arm back and began to step up.

'You gibbin' me cheek?'

He was in my face now, flooding my eyes. He

knocked the torch out of my hand. He clapped his forehead hard against mine and kept it there, continuing to stride forward, pushing me back with his skull.

'You were thmilin' a' me', he said. His breath was drink and cigarettes. 'Think I'm munny? Think I'm muckin' munny?'

His forehead was caving mine, pushing me back and down, back and down. His eyes were forked nothing. I waited for him to cluck his head back and bring the full weight of his skull crunching onto the bridge of my nose. A spurt of blood and agony.

I heard Lisa's voice: 'He's harmless, Teabag. Jesus, he's only harmless.'

I don't know if it was the humiliation of that word, of being named like that before the world, but some flare surged through me in that moment and I suddenly shoved Teabag. I shoved him so hard that he stumbled back over Lisa's knees and fell between the seat rows.

The audience roared as Teabag climbed to his feet. I hunched my shoulders over and raised my shaking arms before my face, like that'd somehow lessen the carnage about to rain down on me. Lisa sprang up between us and spread her arms wide.

'He's not worth it,' she hissed. 'He's not worth it.'

My lip was trembling. Teabag had his shoulders spread, ready to bulldoze me.

'Let's just get out of here, babe,' Lisa whispered to

him, stroking his face. His stare didn't soften, but he didn't make any moves towards me either.

We stayed frozen in that tableau for about eighteen years. Then Lisa stepped backwards, arms open like Christ. She stayed between us as Teabag stalked out the row and down the steps. He almost tore the emergency doors off their hinges on his way out. Lisa followed, carrying their stuff. She didn't look back.

One or two people gave a mocking slow clap as I closed the emergency doors. I was glad the room was dark.

In the foyer, Rachel was already gone. It was just me again. I stood rubbing my forehead, like I'd been marked.

When the movie was over, I turned on the lights, collected the popcorn boxes, and dumped the paper cups. There was a sticky puddle of Coke where Teabag had baptised Duggan. I stood before it for a while. Chest thundering. I thought of leaving the stain there as some sort of gesture. In the end I just mopped it up.

When I finished, I saw I'd a missed call from an unknown number. I thought it'd be Nanny, checking in with me before bed. But it wasn't. It was Rachel.

'Hey Daniel, Rachel here. Duggie's girlfriend... Look, thanks for earlier... Going into that gobshite the way you did was... y'know, fair play, like. Heard you pure faced him down too.'

In the background, I could hear Duggan chant,

'Daniel and the lions!' and Rachel giggled. 'Yeah, you should totally come for a few cans in the woods. A few heads here are moving to Dublin next week too, it'd be good for ye to meet up. So… yeah. Maybe see you later? Sorry if I was mean. Bye.'

The message clicked off. I played it again. Then I hesitated, looking at the dimness of the empty foyer. I texted Nanny.

Few lads at work want to go for pints for my last day

I imagined her and Grandad in the sitting room, delighted I was finally out drinking like some normal young fella. Nanny replied as I typed in the door code outside the Cineplex:

THATS GREAT LOVE DO YOU HAV UR KEY

Before I could answer, my phone buzzed again.

ENJOY URSELF U DESERVE IT HAV A GREAT NITE X

The air was still oven-warm. I would go by the river first. I could still have my little moment, then meet Duggan and Rachel and their whole crew. I saw myself arriving in the woods, already immortalised as the gangly lad who went toe-to-toe with one of the Lyons brothers. It felt like the future and I were somehow turning through one another, already changing our shapes. As I left the cinema I felt ready for almost anything, even the sight of Teabag and Boomerang slouched and waiting for me at the bottom of the steps.

*

Colin Walsh grew up in Galway, Ireland. In 2017, he won the RTE Francis Mac Manus Short Story Award for 'The Flare Carves Itself Through the Dark.' The same year, his other stories were prizewinners in the Bridport Short Story Prize and shortlisted for the Bath Short Story Award and the Aesthetica Creative Writing Award. In 2018, he won the Doolin Writer's Weekend Flash Fiction competition. He has recently been shortlisted for the 2019 Hennessy New Irish Writing Award, and has just had a short story broadcast on BBC Radio 4. He is currently having a nightmarish staring contest with the words that refuse to be his first novel.

Junko Oikawa

Rain

Rain, do not rain...
Soak the dream from the eaves

Anamnesis?

Heap the nights up to the sill,
Sleet in my veins, sleep away the pains

*

Wind, do not sweep...
Crystals in the sky, rosary of tears

Foreordination?

Pearls rolling down to the sleeves,
Scoop the scent in my hands, within a dream

雨音に 夢路はとほく ぬばたまの 夜をしのびて かよふ袖の香

*

Junko Oikawa lives in Brussels. She is an educator and freelance writer.

Dimitris Politis

The Extraordinary Colours of an Ordinary Day

A DAY LIKE ANY OTHER, I glanced at my unwashed and scruffy reflection in the mirror. The intense glare from the hovering halogen spotlights above me, reflected the turquoise of the toilet tiles, blinding my sleepy, half-closed eyes. Antagonised by the intensity of their colour, I stroked my bearded chin with gentle movements.

Like a tsunami of turquoise—couldn't be more '80s...! This bathroom badly needs a makeover, together with the whole apartment! Irrelevant thoughts flashed through my mind while my hand grabbed my razor. As I started to shave with quick, vigorous movements, an inexplicable feeling possessed me. Even though I was still half asleep—40 years had not been enough to cure my early morning allergy!—all my senses felt in a state of high alert.

In complete contrast to other early mornings, I could really smell the perfume of the shaving foam; I heard my warm razor blade decapitating every single hair of my beard like a precise, minuscule, guillotine. The intense colour of the bathroom tiles continued to besiege me relentlessly when I went into the shower, where the abrasive freshness of thousands of water droplets attacked my body.

A while later in the kitchen, the steaming dark liquid that was dripping through the rumbling coffee machine filter like every other day, this time filled my nostrils with an unprecedented, intoxicating aroma. As I rapidly downed huge spoonfuls of unusually flavoursome, crunchy bits of cereal, I checked the colour of the steaming molten liquid out of the corner of my eyes. It seemed more velvety and browner than ever as I filled my cup; my mind fixated on the hands of the clock across the counter.

A quarter of an hour later, I followed my usual routine to the metro. The Brussels sky had already started to light up. Its pale blue was gradually getting brighter, in its timid attempt to mock the colourless apathy of the city, with its dusty tree trunks, sombre buildings, grey tarmac and drab cobblestones, and mousy, mute, silhouettes rushing along the pavements.

With ashen colours of despondency, dejection and indifference everywhere, I escaped down the silvery grey escalators only to find more of the same bleakness further down the platforms: black and grey tiles on the floor and walls, colourless fluorescent lights, matched by expressionless faces.

In stark contrast, the oversweet smell from the

nearby Belgian waffles stand, swamped my nostrils. The usual preoccupations of the day were attacking my brain: estimations and calculations of what awaited me at my desk, absolute priorities and deadlines, urgent emails, papers and procedures. The pale front spotlights of the metro pinned me down like bulging eyes from the depth of the tunnel, interrupting my mundane worries.

The tin-coloured carriage dragged itself hissing in front of my feet. Its arrival hit me with a raw wave of humidity, pungent with the green-grey smell of mould diffused from the dark underground tunnels.

I rushed into the first wagon with a quick leap. The lingering smell of fresh waffles and a place never touched by sunlight was replaced by the odour of the huddle of accumulated morning breath of thick, stale air. I squeezed myself into the first empty corner I could find. A pretty woman in her forties came and stood just across from me. Her bright red coat stood out among the gloomy winter clothing of our travelling companions.

Red glowing ruby, I fixed my eyes on her. The scarlet coat confounded her discreet attitude, and she emanated an air of splendid superiority. It emphasised her lucid, transparent complexion and her lustrous torrent of brown hair in the most flattering way. Absorbed in the screen of her mobile phone, she seemed totally oblivious to the crimson aura she spread around her. An aura that made her shine amongst the passionless, monotonous and colourless mass of the carriage and its occupants.

Seven stops later, I got ready to move to the exit the minute my station was announced on the carriage loudspeakers, in perfect Brussels Flemish: "Maalbeek". Upon the smooth sliding open of the carriage doors, I was one of the first to jump out. With brisk steps, I headed to the nearest escalator. A loud, garbled howl made me stop and turn my head back. My eyes were dazzled by an intense blinding blaze as if they were attacked by a thousand colours; a myriad of molecules from colourful, fragmented glass.

Huge orange ball with a taste of gunpowder, I was assailed by a deafening, rumbling sound, by flaring flames, by a golden burning sensation.

Maalbeek metro station saw a different kind of 'sunlight' that day.

Before I had time to react, I was thrown violently to the platform ground. I found myself lying on my belly, my face pressed against the grimy floor tiles. And then, deadly silence. A thick cloud of dust everywhere, masking an absolute, uncomfortable silence. The astounding reflections of thousands of colours started quickly to lose their brilliance. They slowly turned purple, fading to a tan mass and then disappeared.

Darkness.

I tried to open my eyes. It took a huge effort. White powder and white blur came to replace the blackness. Indistinct, bleached tiled walls all around me. The ruthless attack of the white dust made my eyes sting and smart.

Blinding, brilliant white everywhere, accompanied a terrible, burning sensation in my lower back. And then a cacophony of random noises, of voices accompanied by people frantically running around, dominated the disastrous disorder of the scene. A scene that only a moment ago, expressed a banal, perfectly normal order. Milky shadows, ghosts in the white fog of dust started running right and left in a panic, like mice caught trying to escape from an ashen rat trap. Incomprehensible voices, incomprehensible languages, wild cries and screaming, a desperate baby shrieking, lost in the battered scene. And the white powder, absolute master of the underground chaos always there, ever-present. Together with the turmoil and the fear, still tingling my eyes, making them ache each time I tried to open them.

Is this the white of death? I wondered.

Time passed.

I managed to open my eyes again. No tingle. The atmosphere was now clean, almost dusted. A light, fresh breeze, caressed my face. A sense of relief? Maybe. Lying on my back on a stretcher, I was gazing at the morning sky. A soft, pale blue announced the arrival of spring and revival. Clear and azure, scattered with white cotton puffs of clouds. *Blue serenity.*

I felt a gentle squeeze on my left arm. I turned my head towards it. An ebony-skinned woman, dressed in white, pinned her black velvet gaze straight into my eyes. *White mantle of salvation and hope*.

"My name is Amina, try not to move. We will put you in the ambulance shortly. You will be OK. You were lucky." A dim, worried smile attempted to brighten her preoccupied face. I made an effort to turn my head to her in order to reciprocate. My pain made each movement so arduous, almost unbearable. At the same moment out the corner of my left eye, I caught the person laying on the stretcher next to me: my elegant travelling companion in red appeared to be conscious, communicating with the stretcher carrier. Her crimson coat soaked and splashed all over with garnet coloured stains, accentuated even more by the fluorescent green waste jacket of her saviour. *She is alive*!

Hours later, in my hospital bed, I found myself alone, abandoned for a brief moment by my medical saviours and my preoccupied visitors. Deluged by so many questions, trying to make sense of what had just happened, trying to identify if I felt more angry, confused, desperate or numb.

My heightened state of senses confirmed to me that I was more alive than ever! Elation and gratitude overwhelmed me. Gratitude for the doctors and nurses who were still running distraught outside in the corridors. Gratitude for the strong painkillers that sweetened and almost eliminated the pain, even if temporarily. Gratitude for that feeling of security, the sense of being sheltered and protected in the safe sanctuary of the hospital.

The last bright rays of the day sneaked in through the tenth-floor window. *Orange glow of comfort and relief,* I felt my face lovingly embraced in their warmth. *This day of blasts and noise, of horrid blazes and agonising cries, a veritable Newton's disc with its exuberant colour reflections, proved to be, after all, a day unlike any other...* I focused my gaze on the tangerine brightness that illuminated the west-facing window.

*

Dimitris Politis *was born in Tinos, Greece, and has lived in Greece, Ireland, the UK, Italy, Luxembourg and Belgium. He has written articles and reviews on European working conditions, and published two novels and several short stories in Greek literary magazines, websites and collective publications. His stories have won the Eyelands and Colours literary competitions.*

S.R. Harris

Another Country

In my head I've travelled to this country many times.
Now I wonder where the pictures are that lured me
   here:
the jobs, the shops, the smiling faces.
I cannot read the signs. *Private property.*
Dangerous dog. Keep off the grass.
The rows of houses neatly trimmed,
the parking places for the cars.
Words skulk beneath my tongue.
Can you. Will you. Help me. Find a life.
People turn away. Office hours are from nine to five.
In this world of paperwork
I, who have no papers, am not here.

I didn't think I'd bring my country with me
but it came to visit, uninvited,
wound itself around me like my mother's scarf.
Each night I travel to the village where my house once
   stood.
The brightness of the sky that lights the herd of cows

stumbling through the plains, all skin and bones.
The empty well. The tainted earth.
Nothing grows from gunshot wounds.
In the dust I find a child's hand.

How can I build on other people's bones?
I seek another country where there's room
to breathe, the air is sweet, a scent of lemon leaves.
A door is open. Someone calls my name.

Sightings

For Mum

I search for you in places that we knew.
In the village shop, behind the jars of boiled sweets,
I am growing smaller, hanging on your skirt.
I brush against you in a country lane, a summer sky,
the scent of watermint, a taste of blue.
I do not want there to be nothing left of you.

I come across reminders of your world,
a nametag on a nightdress, a stapled coffee cup.
I taste you in a recipe for treacle tart,
the crumbs of Sunday afternoons.
An inscription in *The Book of Common Prayer*:
'From your loving mother, Xmas 1933'.
Once I caught a glimpse of you in a photograph of me.

You have been silent now for years.
But still I hear your voice in the names of wild flowers,
bird's foot trefoil, hollyhock, forget-me-not.
On leaning down to reach a cowslip on the river bank,
I have felt your hand in mine.

Today I see you standing in a field.
To reach you I must cross a line of silver grass.
The air is thin as thread.
When I get there you are gone.

Back home your grandchildren
are watching telly, listless, bored.
I berate them for not finding something
else to do, sounding just like you.

A Crack

I have no name
no place to go
but if you let me in
I will not weigh you down
or wear you out.

I'll be the lightest part of you,
the edge where air is thin.
The point where land and sea dissolve
beneath the surface of your skin
I'll keep you whole.

I slip inside a crack of doubt,
a door ajar, a window open in the dark.
Like snow I take you by surprise,
thwart your well-made plans,
transform your muddy rivers into glass.

I am the change in you.
The place where you can start again
this winter's night,
a birth, a death,
a donkey's breath.
The chink of light that,
in a twinkling,
turns the straw to gold.

*

Sarah R. Harris has written children's books that have been translated into Dutch, including a series about a sheep called Skye (www.asheepcalledskye.com). Her short stories have been shortlisted for the Bridport Prize and published in Wild Cards: The Second Virago Anthology of Writing Women. She gives poetry workshops, organises open mic evenings, and is working on the novel Plums Taste Different Here.

Aisling Henrard

Lining their Pockets

THE HEADLIGHTS OF THE CARS coming towards her flickered in the pouring rain. Elaine indicated to turn off the main road, into a new-build housing estate. *Tick, tick. Tick, tick. Tick, tick.* Three, four, five cars snaked by. Seeing a break in the streaming traffic, she turned the car into the estate and veered left towards her house at the back. Number 88. *Two fat ladies. Eight-eight.*

Her blue rubbish bin lay in the road where it had fallen after being emptied by the rubbish truck earlier that day. She pulled into the driveway of Number 88, cut the engine and reached into the back seat for her new fold-up umbrella. (*Penneys. Five euros. Thanks!*) She threw her handbag over her shoulder and opened the car door, struggling with the umbrella for a moment before it opened. *Pop!* Running over to the stricken bin, Elaine noticed that someone had run over the edge of her lawn. Muddy grass, tyre tracks. *Tsk...* Probably the postman, the eejit. She never saw him, but, sure, who else?

Dragging the bin behind her, she pulled open the

side gate and pushed the bin into its place at the side of the house. She hit the remote lock button. *Beep, beep! Flash of lights!* The side gate slammed shut behind her, and she rushed to the back door, fumbled with the keys and stepped into the dry back hall. She folded the umbrella. One of the spokes had been bent in the fight with the bin. She threw it onto the pile with five others. Umbrellas for rainy days, a rainy haze, rainy stays. One, two, three, four, five, six. She opened the door from the back hallway to the rest of the two-bedroom, one en-suite, two bathrooms, all-mod-cons estate house.

Once inside, Elaine pulled off her light jacket and hung it in the hall closet with the other winter coats. She heard her waterproof trench mock her from the back of the closet.

'Stupid bitch.'

In the front room she flicked on the big screen TV waiting in the corner. *Click. "Welcome to the real world. It sucks. You're gonna love it!" Canned laughter.* Turning to walk into the kitchen she heard a sound. The cat flap in the back door rocked on its hinges as her cat slunk through. Overfed. Fat. Faaaaaat.

'Hi, puss,' she greeted the cat, bending down to stroke it. 'What were you doing out in this weather?' she asked the creature, wiping the damp from his fur on her trouser leg. The cat ignored her and went straight to its feeding dish, looking back to see if she followed.

'Just a minute, fatty,' she said. Elaine dumped her

car keys and handbag on the kitchen counter and switched on the small kitchen TV, flicking through the channels to the 6 o'clock news. The Angelus was just ending.

'Dong. Dong. Dooooooooooong.' Elaine sang along with the pealing electronic bells.

She crossed herself as she prepared the cat's dinner. Lazy habit.

After tipping fresh nuts into the cat's bowl, she opened the small chest freezer (all mod-cons!) and took out some leftover chicken curry. She put it into the microwave, punching holes in the top with a small, sharp knife, and put the kettle on to boil. Leaving the microwave humming in the kitchen, the television keeping it company, she dragged herself upstairs to change out of her work clothes and into a pair of tracksuit pants.

'The national uniform,' Mairead said at work today. She was from Liverpool, but Elaine had laughed anyway.

The microwave called for her attention as she came back down the stairs, and she dumped the curry on a plate and waited for the boil-in-a-bag rice to cook so that she could burn her fingers on its burn-free packaging.

Plate, a glass of water and Elaine went into the front room to watch TV from the couch. The newsreader, she could never remember his name, was waxing lyrical as she tuned in.

'...list of events for the 1916 rising commemorations to include state occasions and community events across the country.'

Why couldn't she remember his name? She stared at the man, licking a stray piece of rice off her lower lip.

'But one group comprising 850 relatives involved in the rising, says it's boycotting tonight's event because they have not been properly consulted about the plans.'

"Relatives of the Rising." She thought. "Were they all relatives of each other? All 850 of them? No. Relatives of the rising. How well placed did your great-grandfather have to be in the fighting to be counted as a 'relative'? Standing in the GPO beside Collins?! She figured there was probably a sight more than 850 'relatives of the rising.'"

She picked up the remote control and flicked through the channels. David Attenborough droned in elegant tones about the majesty of big cats in the Serengeti. She glanced at the overweight animal wolfing down nuts in the kitchen.

'Huh!' she snorted.

She watched for a few minutes, lifting forkfuls of bland curry and boil-in-the-bag rice to her mouth. Her phone rang.

'Hi, Mam,' she answered.

'Hi, love. How're ya? Did you have your dinner already?'

Elaine put her plate on the floor and drew her legs

up underneath her on the couch.

'Grand, yeah. Just finished. I had some of that chicken curry I made at the weekend. I had left overs in the fridge.'

The cat was nosing around the plate on the floor. She pushed him away with her foot.

'How was work today?'

'Grand, Mam. Same as usual, nothing special. One of the girls is leaving this week, so we have a do tomorrow night.'

She picked at some chicken stuck in her teeth.

'Oh, that'll be nice, a night out with the girls. Where are ye going?'

'Chez Francois,' Elaine replied. 'You know that French place in town. Too fancy for me but you know what the girls are like. Notions. We'll go next door for drinks after I suppose.'

'Ah, you never know. You might enjoy yourself. You never know who you might meet on a night out,' her mother hinted.

Elaine rolled her eyes. She listened. Her mother filled her drifting mind with lists of the town's dead and dying, the misfortunes of the women she met that week at mass, some story about a neighbour's kid who was supposed to have her First Communion on Sunday but had fallen and broken her wrist.

'Have you talked to Brendan today?'

'No, Mam, I haven't heard from him.' Elaine responded to the same enquiry she got every evening about her brother. 'You know he never calls me.'

'Ah, you know how it is with work and the kids and the trial on top of everything. Sure you'll see him at the weekend.'

'What would he want with calling his little sister who only works in a booth and him a big fancy developer?'

Elaine picked up the dirty plate and walked into the kitchen, the phone pressed to her ear. She opened the dishwasher (all mod-cons!), put the plate and cutlery in, added a detergent tablet and switched it on.

'Ah now, Elaine,' her mother chastised her. 'Do you have company tonight?' she continued, failing miserably to hide the curiosity in her voice as she awkwardly changed the subject.

'No, Mam, there's nobody here, that's just the dishwasher and the TV.'

'Ah well, sure you never know with the job going well and the new car, you won't be long picking up a man. Maybe you can have your hair done before you go out tomorrow night. Get them to cover the bit of grey at the roots. You know you should talk to Brendan at the weekend, maybe he could set you up with one of his friends.'

Elaine rolled her eyes towards the lamp on the ceiling. *Ikea. Forty euros. Thanks!*

'Yeah, listen, Mam,' she cut off her mother. 'I have to put out the laundry while it's still dry,' she said, staring out the kitchen at the rain pouring down into the cramped back yard. 'I'll let you go. I'll call on

Saturday before I come home.'

'Ok, love. Have a good night tomorrow night. See you on Saturday.'

'Yeah, tell Dad I said hi. Talk later, Mam. Bye. Bye. Bye.'

She hung up the phone and put the kettle on for tea. Back in the front room, she sat on the couch and picked up the remote control.

'Cover the grey in your hair, arsa Mamai,' she copied her mother's tone exactly. 'Tsk.'

She flicked through the channels.

'Enjoy alcohol respons-'

Click.

'Pets know what they want and-'

Click.

She stopped briefly on an agricultural programme she knew her father would be watching. She considered watching it to have something to talk about on Saturday but kept flicking until she came to reruns of *Friends*. Easy watching. She liked yer wan's hair. She dropped the remote and stretched out on the couch. The cat leapt up beside her.

After the first episode she went out to make a cup of tea. After the second, she sighed and got up off the couch. Pulling on a pair of old runners, she picked up the remote control and walked to the exercise bike in the corner and pulled off the cover. She drew the curtains to hide from the curtain-twitchers across the street.

After a few minutes of pedalling, the TV flickered. Off and on again. Then it flicked off and stayed off. Elaine tried a few buttons on the remote. Nothing happened. She looked down at the remote in her hand, banged it off the handlebar of the bike, all the time pedalling. She looked at TV only to find it had disappeared from her vision. In fact, the entire room had disappeared, leaving only Elaine and her bike, pedalling in a pool of dim light. Where the TV, couch, armchair and windows had been before, there was only a haziness, a foggy darkness. She slowed her pedalling.

A flash of light burned the room from her vision. She raised her hand to shield her eyes. When she lowered it, a moment later, she was sitting on her bike in a plain, white room, in front of a table. There were two people, one male and one female, standing behind the table, smiling inanely. Alarmed, she looked around for an escape. Seeing none, she jumped off the bike, putting it between her and the others.

'Please, Gatekeeper, put down your weapon and sit at the table,' said the female.

Elaine spun in confusion. There was nobody else in the room. There was nothing on the walls, no openings, no windows, not even a door that she could see. The woman approached with her hands outstretched.

'You are welcome here, Gatekeeper, please sit with us. We will not hurt you. Just put down the weapon.'

Elaine looked at the remote control in her hand. She had raised it to throwing height. She lowered her arm, and the woman smiled at her. The man, still standing behind the desk, gestured towards three empty chairs around the table.

'Please. Sit,' he said, smiling.

Elaine approached the nearest chair and sat on the edge, looking around her but mostly at the two individuals who now seated themselves across from her.

'Where am I? Who are you?'

'We are sorry to have brought you here in such a manner, Gatekeeper,' the man began. 'We only wish to ask you some questions about your… role,' he finished.

Elaine furrowed her brows.

'My role? Wait. Is this something to do with Brendan's business?' she asked. 'I know nothing about the loans or the deals,' she said. 'All I know is what they said in the news, nothing more. He tells me nothing.'

The pair looked at each other.

'We know nothing of this Brendan, Gatekeeper,' said the woman. She spoke serenely although Elaine noticed her mouth moved in strange shapes as she spoke, over exaggerating the words like someone speaking to a deaf person for the first time. Like she was testing, tasting the shapes of the words. 'We wish to know more about the place you guard. From whom do you guard? From what do you guard?' she asked.

'The place I guard?' Elaine asked, completely lost.

'Yes, Gatekeeper,' said the man. 'Each day you guard a place and grant others access to it, one at a time. You and the other Gatekeepers. It is a special place, we imagine. We wish to know the purpose of your guarding, if there is something of great value behind your gate.'

Elaine stared at them. She began to suspect it was a practical joke. The guys at work had never pulled one on her, but they were always at it with each other. *Jokers. Messers. Fuckers.*

'The *special* place that I guard?' she asked.

'Yes Gatekeeper.' they replied in unison.

'You mean the booth?!' she asked.

They looked at her with expressionless faces but a hint of bewilderment and frustration around their strange mouths.

'Is this some sort of joke?' When neither of them replied she continued. 'I sit in the booth and take money from people. When they give me too much I give them change,' she said.

'Ah,' the man smiled. 'They must pay to enter this place?'

'Well, yeah,' shrugged Elaine. 'Otherwise they can't get on the motorway.'

'And this motorway is a special place?' asked the woman.

Elaine paused. She sighed, a bit tired after the day at

work. They were getting on her nerves with the ridiculous questions, and she still suspected a trick.

'I dunno. I suppose it helps them to get to the airport faster—it's a direct route—and if they want to go to the Northside without going through town, then the motorway is the best option. The retail park is up there too. That's where I got my sofa last year,' she added. 'Fake leather but you wouldn't know it to look at it. Eight hundred euros. Harvey Norman. There was an option for a matching recliner, but I didn't have the cash. It would have been a pain to drive the whole way through the city centre in that shite van Brendan loaned me, so I took the motorway. Anne took my toll,' she added half smiling. 'And there's a new Ikea just after opening up there too.'

Elaine was beginning to feel comfortable, although she continued looking over her shoulder for the hidden camera or one of the lads from work.

'And all of these... places are special enough to warrant guarding and paid entry?'

'Eh...' she paused, a little unclear on this part. The motorway had been a project during the early 90s and had been well paid for at this stage. Elaine's father regularly went on about having to pay tolls when the roads were paid for twice over. His theory was that the money was really going elsewhere. She picked at some lint on her tracksuit pants (*Penneys in the sale. Five Euros!*) and decided to stick with what she knew.

'Well, you know what the construction companies

are like. Always trying to squeeze the last drop out of us. Lining their pockets with our wages. Brendan included—he's no saint you know. Nobody asked him how they could afford to buy two new cars this year, and that was *after* the company went bust! They're the ones really running the country, let me tell you, telling the ministers what to do, bullying the local councils,' she continued her rant in a more confident tone. 'Dad says we'd all be better off if they were rounded up and pushed out to sea!' she finished. She folded her arms and sat back.

'Listen" she said. "If it's all the same to you, I need to get back. I have to message some of the girls about the do tomorrow night, and I want to wash my hair before I go to bed.'

The others were staring at her in silence. They exchanged a brief look, and the man spoke.

'As you wish, Gatekeeper. You have answered our most pressing questions, thank you. You have been more honest with us than the other gatekeepers.'

Elaine turned around, looking for the exit. Or possibly the aforementioned others.

'How do I….' she began, and the world went blank.

*

Eyes cracked open, just enough to let in a blinding headache. It was worse than the one she had after that hen do last year in Westport, and that had been bad. She rooted around in the drawer of her bedside locker and found a box of paracetamol. Empty. *Fuck*. She groaned as she climbed out of bed. Glancing in the mirror, she ran her hand through her hair. *Hadn't she washed her hair before bed*? Her thoughts were fuzzy. She didn't remember anything after her workout. Chalking it up to a severe migraine, she went downstairs and saw that she had left both TVs on all night.

'Tsk,' she berated herself. The ESB bill was already soaring. Airtricity, or whatever it's called these days. She picked up the remote from where she had dropped it beside the exercise bike. As she raised her hand to switch off the TV, she stopped. The faces on the screen were familiar in the way of all newscasters, but she couldn't place them. Trying to remember which channel they usually appeared on, something the man was saying got through to her fuzzy brain.

'People of Earth. We have your leaders. By noon today you will have surrendered all weapons, codes to nuclear weapons and other means of retaliation. You will allow us to enter your atmosphere. If this does not happen by the appointed time, we shall begin executing your leaders, one at a time, until such time as our requests have been met.'

The image on the screen cut to a live video of a plain, white room with no windows or doors, filled with people. Some were banging on the walls of the room, some were examining the walls trying to find an opening, others were sitting at a small table in the centre of the room. There, sitting in the third chair at the table, with his head in his hands, was her brother Brendan.

The telephone rang. She picked it up in a daze. As she did so, she flicked through the other channels. They were all broadcasting the same image of the CEOs of the world's biggest construction companies, going mad in a plain, white room.

'Hi Mam,' she said. 'I just turned on the TV.

'Jesus, Elaine, what's going on? What the hell is Brendan doing on TV? I thought he did all the interviews for court weeks ago!' Her mother's voice was rising in hysteria.

'Mam, listen for a minute...' she began. Elaine hesitated, staring at the figures, screaming in silence on the screen.

'Promise not to get cross, ok?...'

*

Aisling Henrard: *Irish living in Brussels, Aisling cites public transport as her muse—its wild characters spark her imagination. She feels writing is an itch she has to scratch; the stories keep bothering her until she finally gives in and transfers them to paper.*

Mimi Kunz

The Museum of Favorite Things

WE BOUGHT A HOUSE in Molenbeek. Do you know Molenbeek? It is the fanciest neighborhood in Brussels, which was nominated cultural capital of the Northern United Hemisphere last year (in 2035). Twenty years ago, Molenbeek was run-down, a poor problem area, and a terrorist hideout. They found Salah Abdeslam there—the criminal who was involved in the Paris stadium attacks and got away alive. After his arrest, the community of Molenbeek organized guided tours to re-establish a sense of security, and it worked well. We bought the house just in time and rented it out to some artists. Prices rose, and when they left to live in a cheaper part of Brussels, teachers moved in with a patchwork family, and after them a couple of women. And then Ian and me.

*

I am 60 years old. Today is my birthday. I woke up with *Yesterday* in my mind...*Mhm hm hm hm seemed so far away... why... had to go...* It is my first birthday alone, without Ian, and I make myself a warm breakfast—

tempeh and eggs, tomatoes, beans. Ian hated beans. It is a beautiful morning, and while I prepare my feast, I look out into the garden—a long, uneven, squarish patch of brown-green grass. I sit down at the table by the window.

"I have a song in my head," I would say if Ian were here.

"Yes?"

I would nod. Yes. "*Yesterday.*"

Ian would hum it.

I would smile, put down my fork and raise my mug. "Did you know Paul wanted to call it *Scrambled Eggs*?"

Ian would laugh—quietly. A considerate, blissful laugh. "And now: *Scrambled Eggs* by Paul McCartney," he would say.

"He did!" I put down my cup in order to raise my hands. "He woke up one morning with the melody in his head. He thought it was a song that already existed, and when he realized it didn't, he worked on the melody using *Scrambled Eggs* as a title."

*

I finish my breakfast and tell Ian that I'm off to do some gardening. I don't normally talk to him anymore, but today is my birthday and pretending he is here feels better than accepting that he is nowhere, gone back to nothing. I know that is dead. I am not sentimental. But it is my damn birthday, and no one should have to celebrate their 60th birthday without their lifelong love. So—Ian, here's to you.

Maybe there is a part of us that travels, that is born again as an animal or a plant. I don't believe in it—burial rituals are just stories—but today, more than at Ian's funeral, I wish I were religious.

*

I will plant some artichokes. I walk the length of the garden before setting to work in its centre, pushing the spade into the dirt. The earth is slightly wet and clings to the blade. On my second push, the spade scratches something. I dig on carefully and slowly uncover the form of... a leg! I drop the spade and kneel down, feel in my pockets for my phone. I voice the emergency number, but before I say "call" I close my mouth. The leg looks unused. Artificial. A very good prosthesis, considering it's not bio-printed. I take off my jumper and carefully put the leg on it, then note the date and time and the exact position where I found it on my screen.

"Ian," I say when I carry the leg into the house. "Look." Ian was an anthropologist and the conservation-restoration specialist at the Musical Instruments Museum. I prepare some tea while he inspects the leg, and go back to my artichokes. I hope they will grow this summer. I will sit on my terrace with a glass of wine, listen to the Mauritian orchestra, and eat my homegrown artichokes, dipping the leaves into Kalamatian olive oil. Maybe I should plant an olive tree, too. The spade gets blocked again, and I wonder if the city wall used to be anywhere near here. The obstacle feels softer than stones though, and I put aside my spade and get a small shovel to see what can be done. I scrape and slowly free—a chair.

"Ian!"

*

I work meticulously and in silent concentration. Ian watches me uncover green-golden upholstery and mahogany legs.

"Van de Velde, Art Nouveau," he says, as I carry the chair inside. He gets some books and sits down at the table to check the details while I make sandwiches.

"Should we call somebody?" I ask over lunch and know that we both think of the museum.

"Let me read up on this first, so we know what we've found," Ian says, pointing to his pile of books.

There is not much I can do to help him, and I want to plant the artichokes before it gets dark.

"If you find anything else call me, okay?" he says, and kisses me on the cheek.

The sound of my laughter fills the mild afternoon air. Let's do this, I think, looking at the rooted shoot of the artichoke. But I don't get far.

*

"There is a monitor," I tell Ian, who follows me outside. He kneels down beside me, and I brush away some mud.

"A computer," Ian says. "A Mac."

"What year is it from?"

"I'm not sure. What do you think?"

I put on magnifying glasses for closer inspection. "Maybe 2015, or 2016."

Ian beams at me.

"So, what do we do now?"

I dig deeper. We find a wig, dancing shoes, a watch, a leather jacket, a Chinese coffee table, a fountain pen.

"Would you like a swimming pool?" Ian asks when we have dug the length and width of the garden, standing two meters below the grass line.

"Why not?" I look around. "Or a pond..."

"Or a bunker."

"Or a museum."

"The museum of..."

"Arbitrary objects?"

They are not so arbitrary though, I think, covering Ian's study with tablecloths and putting everything there. The sun has set, and I decide to—

The bell rings, and I open the door to my neighbour Simon. He just came home from work and is wearing a pressure suit. (He is a space traffic director.) His dark skin is shiny with sweat, and he smells good.

"He is young enough to be our son," Ian whispers.

I nod, glancing past Simon at Ian. *"You have to admit he is not at all bad-looking..."*

"Right now he looks concerned I think," Ian says. I shake my head, smiling, and turn to Simon who asks about my garden. I lead him to the study. He takes a good look at the objects, and while he does, I prepare tea.

"They are special things," he says, and takes the cup I hand him. "Thank you."

"They are," I say, offering sugar. "Either unique in a personal way or precious possessions."

He nods, stirring his tea, and I show him the map of where I found what. He wrinkles his forehead, tracing his finger along the edges of my garden. We look at each other, and I nod. "Tomorrow?"

*

Simon calls in sick to work. We take my spade and some shovels and cross the line of bushes that mark the border between our backyards.

By the end of the day, we have retrieved a samurai sword, a coffee machine, an edition of Baudelaire's *Fleurs du Mal*, a bed, a camera, a teddy bear, a wedding dress, and a piano.

"We need to organize a meeting," Simon says, and I agree.

We buy beer, cook rice and crispy crickets, and set up tables and benches in the street.

Everybody who owns a flat in the block shows up. Most of them are curious. Some are alarmed. "We shouldn't let the kids play in the grass. Maybe it's toxic."

"Maybe this used to be a rubbish dump."

"It's not rubbish though. They are objects. Expensive stuff and personal souvenirs."

"Where's Djenabou?"

"Who?"

"She's the local historian."

Djenabou arrives and confirms what we already know. It is not rubbish. But what it is and where it came from she doesn't know.

"Maybe a war site—possessions of prisoners who got killed."

"When do possessions ever get dumped? The Greeks had to leave their golden teeth in Istanbul; the Nazis made soap out of... Anyway: We throw away bodies. Things we keep."

"In bad times. In good times we bury our dead and give away their things."

"Or we keep them as memories."

Nobody wants to talk about death, and so we decide to go on searching, to dig up all of our gardens.

"Did none of you ever plant anything?" I ask.

"Oh yes—but I've got a bad back, so I had my daughter build me a raised bed."

One family has constructed a pizza oven next to their terrace; a man has turned his backyard into a home for gnomes. I was the first one to have dug into the mud.

"Well, we'll see how far it goes."

*

It takes us one week to reach the edges of our territory. We find furniture, paintings, musical instruments, books, clothes, and sports equipment.

"What about underneath the houses?" someone says, and several people hold their breath until

Djenabou shakes her head. "They've been here long before any of this got buried."

"And look at the map," Simon says, holding up the screen on which we drew the gardens marking all the places where we found something. "Nothing was buried close to the buildings."

I look at Djenabou. "What were those houses before they became, you know, just homes?"

The structure of our houses is common enough—facades facing the streets in four directions—their backs fencing a piece of land which is separated into garden patches.

Djenabou shrugs. "I think they've always been homes."

"We should scan the remaining earth for traces," I say. "I mean, how come some book pages are still there?"

"Yes," Simon says. "We have to find out exactly how long ago each item was buried, and how they have been preserved."

"Preserved?" someone asks and giggles.

*

On the next day, while scanning the earth, I find a spoon. A double-sided spoon. I stole it from a museum café during a holiday with Ian. It could be a different spoon, yes. But near it is a glass frame, and in the frame a description of the day I stole the spoon. It was Ian's birthday and our anniversary. We walked through London and kissed in the middle of every bridge we crossed. The wind blew my hat into the Thames, and we went to see *The Sound of Music*.

*

I don't want to show what I discovered to the others. I need time to process what it means, and I want to do so alone. In Ian's study, I pass along the bookshelves looking at the backs of the volumes. His diary stands out because it isn't a real book, just a block of paper.

I sit down at the table and read. I switch on the light. I am getting hungry. And then, there it is:

21.12.2015

A young man approached me at work today—a modern sociocultural anthropologist from New Zealand. He told me about a museum he wants to open, and asked my advice on the preservation of the artefacts. He is interested in possessions of personal value. His museum will display objects alongside a description of their value in the eyes of their proprietor. He showed the first saxophone of a musician, the broken doll of a little boy, the portrait of a collector, the prosthesis of a handicapped person—he has assembled a magnificent array of objects! I asked if I could contribute something, and he agreed to include my favourite thing in his collection.

*

Today is my birthday. I woke up early. There is no chance that I'll fall back asleep, so I switch on the lights and make coffee. It is 4 am and still dark outside. The birds are singing though, and someone wrote on my window: HAPPY B-DAY! in big, colourful letters. I sit down, smiling. Today I am 62. And today, Simon, Djenabou and I, the newly founded Society for Future History, open The Museum of Favorite Things. We have turned what used to be our gardens into a *souterre* hall with a glass roof.

"Our own Crystal Palace," Djenabou jokes as we walk around it that evening, a part of the crowd, champagne in hand. The place looks festive, and so do the visitors who have come to the opening. We watch them looking at all the objects on display, most of which have no accompanying stories as we never found the letters that went with them.

"The man who invented the museum travelled all over the world to study why we keep things," Simon's son Arkady tells a grey-haired man in a dark suit. "And here he collected the favourite possessions of 200 people. But he died before he could find a place to show them in."

"He did?"

Arkady nods. "He got killed on March 22nd in 2016 in a bomb attack at the airport. The things he had collected were still in his friend's garage. But the friend had had to move out of his house, and he buried the objects here, in our gardens!"

"Ah." The old man looks at me, then turns back to Arkady. "And what, do you think, was his favourite object?"

Arkady moves towards a rocking chair, a violin, and points to a telescope. I smile.

"That's a very good guess," Ian says.

*

Mimi Kunz moved to Brussels after a Post MA at the State Academy of Fine Arts Karlsruhe, Germany, in 2015. In 2017 she received the Academy's Alumni Grant and took part in an artist residency in Cairngorms National Park in Scotland. Her latest short story was published in Entropy magazine. Upcoming exhibitions and publications on www.mimikunz.com

Mauricio Ruiz

Leaving Sempoala, 1948

To my mother, Carolina

Your world has come to a stop
The dust, the fields, even the stale
Smell of church you'll miss
Grandma is eager, jealous
In the city slender visions
Dazzle grandfather, women
Smile at the tailored suit, the shoes
He's a catch

Old friends, the tree behind school, what
The future will look like, pulse pulse
Your heart runs fast, but why
Does the city appeal so much? The peasants
No longer knowing how to dream
Lie swollen, forgotten in the streets, by the feet
Of tall corporate buildings

Memories, green mounds of laughter you
Have brought along, kept them close at night
It hurts, saying goodbye, kissing
The baby goats, the birds, only tears
Make your heart fly south
But why is it that only you
Seem to realize that loneliness
Is this place's real name

Two Paths

Perhaps it was the music
The fading light in her voice
Twirling from a thread
Yellow then blue then purple
My heart, my lips had once been warmed
By the passing flight of happiness

Laughter, I felt it, red and sudden, and wings
My smile grew near you
Is it too late to say I was besotted?
Alone
You see me, dream of me
Though it's not my bed
Your body aches for

Faint my voice in winter sounds
An unwanted goodbye that to the sky
The fragile body of a bird has tethered
Two bodies, one soul
Must learn how to accept
That now there's only that, murmurs
A hug that means surrender

*

Mauricio Ruiz *divides his time between Mexico City and Brussels. He's been shortlisted for the* Bridport Prize *and the* Myriad Editions Competition *in the UK, as well as the* Fish Short Story Prize *in Ireland. His work has appeared in publications such as* Clover, Flash Fiction, Red Fez, Literal Magazine, Flanders Today, The Bulletin, Chilango, *among others. His stories and poems have been anthologized in* All The Ways Home *(Grimbold, 2014), and* North of The Sun, South of The Moon *(Grimbold, 2013). His second collection of stories,* Silencios al sur, *(Ediciones Felou) came out in 2017. He has been granted a residency at Art Omi Writers, New York, to work on a novel.*

Joost Hiltermann

Kawa's Calvary

In 1988, Kawa was a Kurdish villager who got caught up in events beyond his control. Four years later he is living in a camp for displaced people in northern Iraq, where he meets a human rights investigator who has come from America. They go to a hotel in a nearby town, where, in a private room, he delivers a startling testimony.

In his account, here excerpted, he earlier described how, as an army deserter, he was hiding out in the Kurdish countryside east of the town of Kirkuk, mingled in with Kurdish partisans fighting the regime of Saddam Hussein. Then, one day, he now recounts, the Iraqi military launched a major assault.

A Kurdish Displaced People Camp in Northern Iraq, Summer 1992

SITTING IN OUR CAVES, my mates and I, we thought we'd grown accustomed to the shelling. The whistling of shells, the roar of airplanes, the whap-whap-whap of helicopter blades, the impact of explosions, the clouds of dust rising from the earth, spreading all around. We had long abandoned our homes for the safety of these caves, but it's not as if these things have doors that you can shut to keep out strangers, or unwelcome visitors such as dust clouds. That stuff would penetrate our eyes, our noses, our mouths, everything. We were choking and coughing and gulping down water—when we had any—and just trying to stay alive. The nights would bring respite. We loved the nights—except for the bitter cold. We had to be careful with fires, not to attract the pilots' attention, but mostly they left us alone at night. For all the lethality of their firepower, their ability to use it against us was limited to daytime.

Ah, those nights. Don't imagine large caverns with lightbulbs dangling from the ceiling. No such thing. A hole in the ground or a hollowed-out rock surface, fitting ten, fifteen men at most; uneven ground that was hard to sleep on; extreme cold, especially when we could not light fires; no mattresses and sometimes not enough blankets to go around; and the ever-present risk of being fired upon when we went out to gather wood or walked to the village to pick vegetables or retrieve pieces of clothing. Yet what we lacked in comfort we made up for in camaraderie: I made my best friends during those days and nights in the caves! Of course, they are all gone now.

There was Hameed, an army buddy from Kirkuk I had spent time at the front with. He was the joking type, always ready to see the humour in whatever new disaster came our way, always extracting a smile where otherwise we might have grimaced or groaned. There was Mohamed, my cousin. Mohamed "the Taciturn," we called him. Quiet he may have been, but steady as a rock. I could always count on him, in the toughest of times, and this was such a time.

Even if we had grown used to the constant barrage, nothing could have prepared us for what they had in store for us. It all started the hour before sunrise. Hameed poked me in the ribs, trying to rouse me from my rocky bed: "Kawa! Guys! Listen up!" We all could hear it: the distant rumble of airplanes, that oh so familiar sound, growing closer. We jumped up and barely had the chance to splash water on our faces from the handful of buckets we had managed to haul up there the previous night, before we heard the first bombs hitting the ground, their impact muffled still, but approaching with every passing minute. It seemed, from our limited vantage point inside the cave, that the sky was filled with flying craft. We couldn't go out to see nor determine which area they were targeting: our village, or the next, or the one beyond that. Were they going after the local partisan stronghold two valleys over? That would make sense. But this attack seemed louder, bigger, more dangerous than anything we had experienced so far.

By mid-morning, the bombing and shelling suddenly let up. You couldn't imagine the quiet. Yet, it wasn't quiet. Somehow the deafening thuds of the explosions had concealed the sounds of other happenings more ominous still: the screaming of children, the tat-tat-tat of gunfire not far off, the thudding of shells striking the rocky soil further down, in the area where I thought the partisans were, some distance still from us.

And then the exodus. Any creature with legs was moving: men, women, and children, bringing along their goats, their chickens, their dogs…. up, up, up against the steep slopes of the rugged mountain that housed our cave and many others, into the few trees still left standing, to the very top in search of protection—what protection!?—away from the approaching gunfire, with everyone shouting, screaming, crying, cursing in a clatter of hysteria, panic, and fear. Almost mechanically, Hameed, Mohamed, and I were running with them, unable to resist it, as if part of an unstoppable force, scarcely looking back, too frightened to want to see who or what was coming after us.

*

Please, could I have a glass of water? I've been talking so much, my throat has run dry. Just give me a minute to catch my breath. I want you to hear this in full. You haven't heard even a tenth of it. The world's got to know, all of it.

Thank you.

You will tell my story, right? Mine and that of our people? It's all one story, really, with many different strands, all leading to the same end. Except mine. That's why I've been able to tell it. I guess you could call me lucky, but if this is lucky, I'd like to see a poor unlucky bastard dragged down by the weight of this world, and compare notes.

*

We all spent that night huddling amidst the rocks on top of that mountain, wide awake, alert, famished, craving water, consumed by fear and paralyzed by uncertainty. Not knowing what would come next was the worst of it. We let our imaginations run wild, fed by rumours from a man who said he had seen tanks coming up the road from Kirkuk to a woman who claimed soldiers had massacred villagers in a place half an hour's walk from here.

(But how could she know this? Had she been there at the time and somehow, as bombs and rockets rained down, found her way back here? I didn't ask. Nor did I think about it. It occurs to me now, but now, what does it matter?)

Not long after morning broke, everyone started moving down the mountain, and without anyone assuming leadership or taking any kind of express decision. We all just got moving, down the dirt track toward Kader Karam, the nearest town, to surrender to the army, amnesty or not, whatever would happen to us. My friends and I deliberated among ourselves as we started to make our way downhill. We knew very well what awaited us if the amnesty proved to be phony, like so many before it. But during the early hours, in a brief let-up in the attacks, some men we knew, the fathers of some of my deserter friends who had moved to the resettlement camp earlier, came toward us saying: "The army has declared a general amnesty, so don't worry, surrender now, say you're not one of the partisans but a cook pressganged into their band to fix their meals, or something like that!"

I felt reassured, but only a little. We were so exhausted and physically weakened that we could easily agree among ourselves—without exchanging many words—that the best thing would be to chance it: anything except staying in the villages and caves if rural life amounted to daily bombardments, growing deprivation, and a nagging uncertainty about the future. In such conditions, it would be far better to bring that future forward.

As we made our way down, a single human mass stumbling through the brush—people from other villages now joining us, some men driving their tractors, others herding their flocks ahead of them, and everyone carrying on their backs whatever belongings they had found time to collect from their homes, crying babies in their arms, crying children clinging to their sides, everyone else ashen-faced, stunned, walking westward as if guided by an invisible hand—we saw no soldiers. It was a crisp spring morning, just after *Nowroz*, our New Year's, but there was nothing to celebrate. This was more like a funeral procession, except for the palpable fear coursing through the crowd, the contagious sense of anxiety gripping us all. What would be next?

Well, next came not the army but our 'donkey' friends, as we called them: the men the regime called 'Knights.' They were waiting for us on the outskirts of town. "Over here," they yelled. "Have no fear! There is an amnesty, thank God, and thank our Great Leader, May God Protect Him. He's giving you a free pass. Come to us; we'll take down your names. If you have a gun, give it to us, and we'll take you to be resettled. If you are a deserter, the army will detain you, yes, but for three days only. They will put you through your paces and then send you back to your units. That's a hell of a lucky break for you! They could have killed you all. Did you see their weapons? Did you see their bomber planes? They have special munitions, too, they told us, of the type they used in *Halabja*. You guys are lucky you're alive and getting another chance. So, hop hop!"

I wasn't so sure about all that, but what choice did we have? Our time of freedom had come to an end. The partisans, those brave souls who had promised to deliver us from Saddam, had demonstrated they couldn't even so much as protect us from his war machine in our homes. Instead, they had brought the regime down on us by provoking it: by using our lands as launching pads for their nightly attacks on its checkpoints and police posts. Had they ever considered the possible consequences? Had they been so confident of their own strength that they reckoned they could liberate our lands, march on Kirkuk, dislodge Ali Hassan al-Majid from his palace, and send him packing back to Baghdad without resistance, without reprisal, without bloody revenge?

What happened next was that the militia guys brought a lot of Toyota Landcruisers into that area—a reward for their loyalty—and started to hustle us inside. Me and my friends that is. The women and children, they took them elsewhere—where we could not see.

For us this was the first step in the process we expected of being reunited with our units and dispatched back to the front to die in the war—this stupid war of the regime's own making that it wasn't winning, not with all its chemical weapons or with us, its useful cannon fodder.

It was tight in that donkey Landcruiser, but nothing we weren't used to. You think the army is a joyride? In a way, now that we had made the decision to give ourselves up and were on our way to the familiar, we felt relief. And so, we started joking with each other, Hameed especially, taking care not to irritate our escorts. They, however, went out of their way to reassure us, telling us: "You'll see, it'll be over in a couple of days, and then it's back to the army with you guys. If you were smart, you'd try to join our group. It's an easy life, all things considered. Guard duty, mostly, close to home. Sure, we come under attack from the partisans, those traitors you guys are consorting with. What are you hoping to get from them, anyway? What do they give to you? Look, you guys are nearly starving, and shivering from fright. Where will that get you? And now they're going to ship you back to the war, while you could be just like us, driving a Landcruiser!"

They would go on like this as we drove down the dirt road to Kader Karam. I knew exactly where they were taking us: to the army's 3rd Corps command, just outside of town. I knew it well enough. This was an army unit from somewhere in the south: poor fellows who were, in their own way, also victims of the regime. But, dressed in army uniforms, they used their power to humiliate us. And their commanders weren't from the south but from Mosul and Ramadi. They were hardcore. Still, I was prepared for this. I knew the army inside out. As long as you followed their orders, and joked around a bit during the quiet moments, and offered a cigarette or two to your sergeant, you could survive the experience.

After we entered the base, soldiers came, ordered us out of the cars and told us to sit on the drill ground. Our 'donkey' friends, they chatted with the soldiers a bit, then jumped into their Landcruisers and hightailed it out of there. An army officer emerged from one of the barracks carrying a notepad and began to rattle off the names of the villages in the area, and placed the men from each village in separate groups. Then he started to go around. When he came to ours, he asked us for our names and inquired if we were deserters, if we had been with the partisans, and where were our weapons. Of course, I told him: "Yes, I am a deserter. I left my unit last year. But no, I have nothing to do with the partisans; not my kind of thing. I am a farmer, simply trying to stay alive. I don't have a weapon either." The officer was speaking in Arabic, which I understood well, having served in the army, but many of my friends barely got what he was saying, and simply repeated what the man before him had said.

I don't know if my answer satisfied him. He seemed not to care. He never even asked me to which army unit I belonged. I wish I could have seen what he jotted down in his logbook. Not much, as far as I could tell. Just a mark here and a mark there. Would these simple marks determine the fates of me and my friends?

This business done, they put us in army trucks and drove us ten minutes down the road to the police station, in the centre of town. I had been inside it once—a scrappy little place—to renew my driver's license. You couldn't get anything, not even a driver's license, without doing them a favour in return: either a piece of information that would incriminate your cousin or your friend, or a bribe. Sometimes, a pack of cigarettes was enough. I found it odd they would bring us here: why, if we were going to be sent back to our units? It made little sense. And there was no way to get an answer. If we so much as tried to say something, a police officer would hurry over and raise his club.

They ordered us to sit down in the courtyard and "Stay!"—like dogs. Stay we did, for two days and nights without food or drink, not even a sip of water. This was torture, but we reckoned it was our punishment for deserting, and we took heart from the donkeys' words earlier, when they urged us to turn ourselves in: "Three days' detention, and then off to the front with you!"

On the morning of the second day, as we were sitting there, slumped over onto each other's shoulders as we dozed, we were startled by the sound of a helicopter approaching. It circled overhead as if looking for a place to land, like the hawks in the mountains, searching for prey, then plunging down to make their kill. It felt like that, because who knew what that hellish machine was after? We used to be its prey, back in the village, and would save ourselves by scurrying beneath boulders and trees.

I couldn't believe it: it landed right next to the police station, close to where they had made us sit. Out came a man I recognized immediately, and that everyone recognized, because we had seen him on TV: Ali Hassan al-Majid, the man himself! Short, with a course countenance, rat's eyes, and a large bushy moustache like Saddam's. And right behind him, General Bareq, commander of the 1st Corps, tall, imposing. There was a third man, too, a high-ranking officer who from his insignia appeared to be from Military Intelligence.

If I hadn't known Ali Hassan's face before, I would have learned it right there and then, because a whisper went around the courtyard, starting with the police officers and spreading like wildfire: "Sir Ali! Sir Ali!"

That name, that face....it sent shivers down our spines. This man was a butcher, we knew. He had slaughtered many. What was he doing here? He walked in front of us; I could have touched him. At one point he kicked a guy, I'm not sure why, just kicked him viciously in the side. The man shrieked, doubled over. We all sat still as rabbits, hyper alert, frozen, vulnerable, terrified. Fortunately, he did little else. But a video crew filmed the whole thing. They first had us all sitting, then standing in a line, and finally sitting again, with our hands placed behind our heads in surrender. And that was it. They left as swiftly as they had come.

The next morning—mind you, we still hadn't eaten a thing, or received a drop of water—they placed blindfolds over our faces and herded us into waiting trucks. They tied them really tight, those blindfolds, with a knot in the back. I couldn't see, when they came, what sort of cloth this was, but the smell of it startled me, brought me close to fainting. I could imagine where they had gotten these. But at the time, I had no time for imagining other than to think of what the future would bring.

This was the third day of our ordeal, and we were counting on this being the day we would be sent back to our units. To be blindfolded was, therefore, a most alarming turn of events. Some of my friends, Mohamed among them, started to pray, expecting the worst; others, like me, tried to find an explanation for the shift to being treated like ordinary criminals. Perhaps we were to undergo further punishment before being taken to the front—the ultimate punishment, in our eyes—so as to discourage further desertions? Perhaps we were criminals to the police, and they were handling us their usual way, but following the videotaping, we would now be returned to the army, and soon we would be back to being standard deserters—deserving a beating at most but indispensable if this wretched war was to be won. "As long as they don't make us eat these blindfolds," Hameed said, but this time his joke fell flat.

Our onward journey now was a little confusing, not in the least because we couldn't see. Were they taking us to Kirkuk? To Chamchamal? And then where? We didn't know, but after about an hour we stopped and were shoved out of the back of the truck. My blindfold slipped off as I scrambled to my feet, but someone cursed and kicked my legs from underneath me, and I fell, a sharp pain shooting through my every limb. In that brief moment before a soldier tied the cloth again, I could see we were back in a military camp. But which one? They all look alike. Soon another soldier roughly pulled my arms behind my back and placed plastic cuffs over my wrists. From the sound of it, the same was happening to those around me: a lot of moaning and grunting, though no one spoke a word. I was weakened by hunger and utterly terrified.

An officer took down our names—again—kicking each one of us as our turn came: "Your name? Your village? Profession? Saboteur? Were you armed? What did you do for them?"

How to answer such questions? I had to deny any association with what they referred to as the saboteurs, because I knew that surely then I would die. Yes, I had had a weapon. Who didn't in those days? But I couldn't say to them I had one because I belonged to a 'support unit.' To them, it would have meant I was a partisan, while to me it meant that by agreeing to defend my village I could keep it safe from any threat. Such subtleties would be lost on these soldiers, who had no understanding of our situation and neither the training nor the inclination to find out. So I told him: "My name is Kawa; I'm an ordinary villager, but yes, I deserted from my unit some months ago—that terrible war, I couldn't stand it any longer; I left my weapon with my unit when I went on furlough; I'm unarmed, as you can see; I just wanted peace and to go back to farming, my profession. But now I'm ready to go back to the army and serve our Great Leader; May God Protect Him."

He hardly seemed to pay attention to what I said.

Again, a couple of strokes with the pen, that was all, and "next!"

I heard Hameed give in, confessing after several kicks, which elicited from him as many yelps, that, yes, he had been with the partisans, but only as a cook and only because they had given him no choice: "If you don't cook for us, we'll kill you and make life difficult for your family!"

A cook! Wouldn't you know it? I could have written the script.

Hameed's 'confession' was sure to further solidify the picture these soldiers had of the partisans as bloodthirsty marauders. The image conveyed on television and in the newspapers, was of callous, power-hungry mafia bosses who had cynically aligned themselves with the mortal enemy Iran with the intent to kill as many Iraqis as possible in an effort to bring down the Exalted Baath Party and its Eternal Leader, Saddam Hussein, May God Protect Him.

To me, our leaders were noble in their intentions but not so successful in carrying them out. Just look at my situation there and then.

In any event, it appeared to make no difference whether we told the officers we were cooks, hairdressers or personal servants to the partisans, or that we had no association with them whatsoever. Following the cursory interrogation, Hameed and I were not treated any differently, and the same was true for all our mates herded into that army camp that day. In any event, our joint fate not long thereafter showed that the regime considered all of us 'saboteurs' and 'Iranian agents.'

We were hauled back into the trucks, accompanied by kicks and curses, the standard fare. And off we drove again, though not for long. Suddenly we heard many voices—of men, of women and children. We had arrived in town. But which one? I later learned it was Chamchamal. Those people were shouting: "Where are you taking them, our men, our sons? They have done nothing wrong. Let them go!"

As we progressed through the streets, crawling along, the throng appeared to grow, because the number of voices increased, reaching a crescendo. We stopped, and the people now converged on the trucks, on us. Suddenly: the crackle of gunfire, screams. The crowd backed off, but the din barely let up, turning a small protest into an uprising aimed at freeing us from our captors. I heard a thud, and another one as two of my companions jumped out of the back of the truck, and the cheers of the crowd that received them. A third managed to join them, and I was just moving to the back to follow their example, yelling to Hameed and Mohamed, "Let's go!", when the truck staggered into gear, throwing me, and all those who remained, against the floor, and off we were again. More gunfire! More screams! And the women's high-pitched ululations urging the men to battle.

Then: gunships overhead, firing rockets. Everything

dissolved into panic, and we drove off, the noise growing fainter with every screeching turn.

How many died in this foolish act of bravery? Later, my relatives in Chamchamal told me twenty. Or fifty. No one really knew.

*

Could I have another glass of water, please? I'm so thirsty. Thirstier perhaps than I was when all of this happened to me. Or so it seems to me now. And then I'll tell you the rest.

*

Joost Hiltermann, *a researcher and non-fiction writer in professional life, has traveled to many parts of the Middle East, including northern Iraq, where this story is situated. Having reported on historical events there in various outlets, he hopes that a fictionalized account will draw a more diverse audience. If we are to be an international community, tragedy must be shared.*

Cynthia Huijgens

The Things We Do For Love

THE WALL WAS A DIZZYING collage of photographs, flyers and business cards, pasted one on top of another such that words, colors, and images blurred into a single mind-boggling pattern. It was a directory of who's who in the fishing community of Kenai Peninsula and where I was told I could find a charter for hire.

Several bent corners and torn away pages lifted and rattled after someone propped open the door to the bar. The cool, salty sea air pressed against my face and cleared away the cigarette smoke that smelt like it'd been hanging around since yesterday. I stood with a beer in my hand staring out the entrance, mesmerized by the sounds of distant fog horns and the ha-ha-ha of gulls fighting overhead. I turned my attention back to the wall. Tomorrow would come soon enough and I had a big job to do.

The first flyer I read promised "a true Alaskan adventure, halibut fishing at its best!" Below the name Clark Charters was a photograph of two twenty-something guys, nearly identical in appearance but for one receding hairline, standing shoulder-to-shoulder with a stringer of fish stretched between them. Their smiles attracted me instantly. That could be David and me. I pulled the flyer from the wall and stuffed it into my pocket.

When I got back to my hotel room I called Clark Charters and had a brief conversation with a boy who sounded about ten years old. He seemed to know a lot about fishing and assured me Captain Clark knew where the really big fish were. 'It'll be awesome,' David convinced me. By the end of the call I had committed to a full-day charter.

The next morning I woke early and walked to the dock, nervous about my plans for the day. This whole trip had been David's idea. Since his death I'd taken on all the things he didn't get the chance to do. I'd ridden a motorcycle around the Grand Canyon, spent a day buying coffee for random people and asking them to share what they hated most about their bosses. I'd learned to surf in Portugal, and eaten fried bugs rolled into a breakfast burrito while backpacking through Canyon del Sumidero in Mexico. Now I was about to go halibut fishing in Alaska, the one but last item on his bucket list. My love for my brother spurred me on when, like now, I was tired and didn't want to go along with the plan.

Clark's flyer had described "Little Hooker" as a sea-ready nineteen-foot walk-around with inboard motor and aluminium platform off the back. At first glance, all the vessels lining the dock fit that description. I shifted the straps of my backpack that was too heavy with water and snacks, sunscreen and extra layers of clothes, wondering if I'd beat Little Hooker to the marina. After a short walk, I found her tied-up at the end of the dock.

The boat looked like it had seen a lot of action. Her sun-bleached deck was lined by two vinyl benches running the length of the boat on each side. The hull was spotted with rust and missing paint. A once-white cooler sat behind the captain's chair, four fishing poles leaning against the windscreen. It wasn't exactly a walk-around; the bow was accessible, but only by climbing up and over the dash and through a small, hinged window. From a six foot tall flag pole at the stern, a paper bald eagle kite soared on a constant north-easterly breeze.

A man approached from behind carrying a plastic bucket of bait. He walked past without saying a word and boarded Little Hooker. I watched as a boy climbed into the back of the boat, a metal tackle box in his hand. He set the box down and began rummaging around for something inside. I stepped forward.

"Hi, I'm Guy. I think we spoke on the phone?" The boy turned his face to me, but kept his body busy.

"I'm Daniel, but everybody calls me 'Boy,' he said, pulling pliers from the box. The old man clambered from the boat.

"Hi. I'm Guy," I said, unable to hide the nervousness

in my voice, a small tremor in my hand as I thrust it between us.

"You ready to go halibut fishing, Guy?" Clark asked, his hands stained with blood.

Now would be a good time to go, I thought, *if you had any reservations*. I was, of course, talking to David in my head. *What if the engine fails, or we don't catch any fish, or what if this guy is some sort of maniac killer?*

'We didn't come all this way to bolt now,' David said. I felt his warm, reassuring hand on my back.

David was two years older and seemed to relish his big brother role. He could get me to do just about anything. He'd been the one to show me how to ride a bike, master a tre flip on his skateboard, and sneak out of the house without being missed. He was clever and brave, while I was the 'wuss' of the family, the one other kids called 'chicken'. Without David I was nothing. I glanced around at the other boats and the crews busy tending them. Little Hooker was set to be the first boat out. I took in a deep breathe, *This is for you Bro*.

"I'm ready to catch some fish," I responded calmly, trying to wish away the uncertainty hanging around my head like the last patches of morning fog. I climbed into the boat and plunked my backpack onto one of the benches. Two seconds later, Clark turned the engine over. After a brief check of the dials, we set sail. I could see David sitting opposite, rubbing his hands together in anticipation, his eyes arched over an ear-to-ear grin.

We slowly motored our way out of the marina, past hundreds of small and medium sized recreational boats moored along both sides of our path. I took photos of sea stars clinging to rocks and dock posts. They were bigger than any I'd ever seen, some with more than sixteen arms. A minute later we cruised by large commercial fishing trawlers, some nothing more than abandoned, rusted ghosts of their former selves, their tangled cables and fishing nets shimmering in the mist. At Land's End, just before we turned out of the marina, we passed a fish processing plant where hundreds of sea gulls and bald eagles and other shore birds fed from a heap of fish remains. It was an ear piercing, squawking, screeching aviary battle ground, and the stench of rotting carcasses was the worst smell I'd ever encountered. As Clark accelerated into open water, I settled into my seat and took in the fresh air.

Homer Spit disappeared behind us, a brown smudge floating above a vast, blue glassy seascape. My earlier hesitation about Clark and his boat was replaced by a wave of euphoria. I began to fantasize about the fish I would catch, a full stringer like the one on the flyer. I wanted David to be impressed.

As the boat hummed along, I took photographs of birds and watched with encouragement as they flew effortlessly into the sea, emerging time and again with small fish trapped within their beaks and talons. Otter occasionally popped up and rolled onto their backs, clutching an urchin or clam in their webbed feet. I heard the spray from a whale's blow hole, though the large beast evaded my waiting camera.

The morning sun crept above the mountain tops, bright but not warm. I pulled a windbreaker from my pack and zipped it to the end. David began laughing, teasing me about how over-prepared I was, how protective I'd become. He's pestering me, asking, 'are we having fun yet,' and egging me to describe the fish I was going to catch, pointing to every distant mountain range and seal-covered outcrop saying, 'Can you believe it?'

As I relaxed into the bench, the remoteness of Kachemak Bay stirred something deep inside me. To get here I'd flown on two crowded airplanes from Tuscon to Anchorage, then rented a car and driven more than 200 solitary miles south to Homer, "The Halibut Fishing Capital of the World." I was at the end of the end of the road. 'We passed the westernmost point of the national highway system miles ago, Brother. You're way beyond the end of the road, you're out at sea now.' David was right, we were nearly into the Pacific Ocean "where all the big fish will be," he smiled.

David had taken days to explain how I should carry out each item on his bucket list, going over every detail time and again. I agreed to take it on, not fully understanding what it would mean for me. No matter how you prepare, it's never enough. You can never know how you're going to manage without someone who's been there with you since the beginning. At least I had David's instructions, or guidelines, to live everyday by. But I was nearing the end of the list and worried about what would come next.

Boy rose and came to sit beside me. "You okay, Guy?"

"Couldn't be better." I said as I crossed my arms and smiled into the wind.

"We thought you looked sad, so I came over to check on you." He fidgeted and looked back to Clark. "It won't be much longer. Captain wants to be sure we're far enough out-"

"Where all the big fish will be?" I laughed. "I can't wait. I plan on catching as many fish as I'm allowed." I shot a glance at Clark. His long, spindly finger tips stroked the length of his mustache and beard, pulling a few springy, rogue hairs into line.

"I'm feeling pretty good about my prospects. It's such a privilege to be here." I looked out at the rocky coastline dotted with nesting birds. "You're so lucky to live here. I don't even know how to describe it." The scenery was so achingly beautiful I wanted to slip under the water like a playful otter and be lost among the sea urchins forever.

"I've never lived any place else. This is all I know." Boy's eyes searched up a craggy gorge cut deep into a mountain that stretched down to water's edge. "I get to fish a lot, and hunt for clams and moose and bear. It's a pretty good life, I guess."

"Do you live with Captain Clark?"

"You mean Grandpa?" Boy laughed. "Nah. Me and my mom live next door, along with two super annoying sisters and a baby brother named Jack. He's still in diapers."

The engine cut.

'It's show time!' David was eager to catch fish.

Boy dropped anchor then came back to give me a brief tutorial on how to properly hold a ten foot rod, and how to thread two-inch salmon bait onto a very large hook strung ahead of a four-ounce weight. Without a word, Clark fixed my pole and showed me how to set the line. I made myself comfortable on the vinyl bench towards the back of the boat, shifting the rod from hand to hand until it felt secure. I scanned the area for fish. That's when I noticed what looked like green sprinkles on the surface of the water slowly moving with the current.

"Next time, tell your mother to fix you a proper breakfast." I heard Clark bark. I turned to see Boy's head dangling over my side of the boat and another wash of sprinkles came my way.

"Captain, will this have a negative effect on the fish?" I asked, perhaps a little too naively.

"Halibut are bottom feeders Guy. Let out more line if you want to catch one." Clark reached an arm out to pat the back of Boy's head.

While my back had been turned, the slack in my line spun and curled. Embarrassed, I flicked the pole tip upwards, reeling like a madman until I felt the drag of the weight again. The slack returned, and I tried again to land the weight on the sea floor. All I had was my sense of touch to guide me.

"Here, I'll show you. I'm pretty good at this." Boy appeared over my shoulder.

"Are you sure? I don't want you to help me if it makes you sicker." I smiled at his unnaturally green tinted lips.

"I'm over it. I shouldn't have eaten all those damn donuts." Boy took my pole into his own hands and smiled, a hint of green clinging to his teeth and gums.

"Okay Guy, watch this. What you need to do is let out enough line so you feel your weight hit the bottom. Then, once you feel the bottom, lock your reel nice and tight and just check your line every once in a while. Make sure that weight is sitting nice and steady on the bottom. If you feel any pull, or any movement at all, give a tug, like this. And that's how you hook a fish." Boy smiled widely this time, all evidence of sickness gone from his mouth. He handed the pole back to me.

"Now we sit and wait." Boy pushed his bum onto the bench opposite me, opening an old tear in the vinyl.

"Oh, did you see that?" I felt a tug on my line, then another. Boy laughed.

'Tug back,' David said.

"I think I have something," I struggled to keep a grip and surprised myself with the very thought of having a fish at the end of my rod.

"Here, let me see." Boy took my pole and stood with his legs apart in a fortified stance. I watched him strain to pull the rod over his head, reeling in the line as quickly as his hand could turn the crank. His eyes nearly popped from their sockets and he screamed, "Fish on!" Clark came up behind Boy and they wrestled with the pole for a few seconds.

Thrusting the pole back into my hands, Clark said, "This is your fish. You bring it in."

With no time to think, I jumped from my seat and gripped the rod. I tried to remember everything Boy had said about how to catch a fish, but I couldn't remember that he'd said anything about how to land one.

"What do I do now?" I screamed, instinctively pulling the rod back as far as I could, then whipping the reeling around and around as I lowered it back to the water.

"Keep doing what you're doing," Clark said as he lit a cigarette and returned to his captain's chair. Boy stood beside me smiling, giving two 'thumbs-up' and behind him David was doing the same.

The fish gave nothing away, forcing me to use my entire body to hold the line. I pulled and stretched, pulled and stretched. There was a moment when I thought I'd lost it, that it'd somehow slipped from the hook and was swimming around the sea laughing about how it got away. But then it violently yanked the line. I answered with more punch, and soon we were in a sparring match. I refused to give up, even when my arms and legs began to quiver and my fingers went numb. I looked to see that I was still holding the rod then looked back where my line entered the water. The fish remained out of sight, but the line was taunt.

"How long will this take?" I directed my question to Clark. When there was no reply, I looked to Boy. His entire face changed as he came up close and whispered into my ear.

"If you can't do it, he'll cut the line." Clark sat sharpening his pocket knife on a piece of pumice he dipped into the sea from time to time. His wiry hair lifted in the breeze giving him a crazed castaway look.

Frustrated, I sat back on the bench only to discover I had no leverage. I watched in horror as the rod sprang from my hands. "Argh!" I screamed, then immediately scrambled after it. The reel caught between the bench and the edge of the railing. *Quick reflexes David. It's just like you to be here when I fuck up, bailing me out, giving me a second chance to get it right.* I quickly grabbed the rod and didn't even bother looking in Clark's direction. There would be no cutting the line today. Hell or high water, I was going to bring this fish in.

I reeled and pulled, asking Boy to bring me water. He helped remove my windbreaker and roll up my sleeves when I couldn't take the heat anymore. The fish came close, darting towards me, then flipped its white side up before disappearing under the boat. Over time I developed a steady rhythm, pulling in line as fast as I could for one minute, then resting for two. After an hour the fish was beginning to tire. I was tired too, but I was going to see it to the end. David's words encouraged me, 'Focus on what you need to do, and soon you'll feel proud of what you've accomplished'.

Nearly another hour passed before the fish was close enough to grab. Clark took out his gaff hook and while I held my rod steady, he pierced the fish through the lip. Boy came up beside me with a pistol in his hand.

"Take it." Clark barked at me, the strain of the fish pulling his body towards the water.

"I've never used a gun before," I cried. I'd never even held one. Despite the pistol's compact size, I was surprised by its heaviness. My fingers were reluctant to grip the handle.

"No experience required," Clark said flatly, "just don't shoot the boat."

Clark had spoken fewer than two dozen words to me since we launched. I quickly discovered that when he lit a cigarette and stared into the sea, he was reading the water. When he stroked his beard, he was amused by something either Boy or I had said. The long stretches of stubborn silence and penetrating sideways glances expressed so much more than any words he could have uttered. But now he was shouting at me.

"Do it!" I pinched my lips together and gripped the revolver with both hands. I slid my right index finger through the trigger guard and fixed the gun between the eyes of the fish. Sweat dripped into my left eye.

"Closer, Guy!"

I took a step, pushing the barrel into the slippery, brown skin. The fish slapped its tail on the boat, splashing water into Clark's face. I had assumed the halibut would go limp once it'd been hooked but instead it continued thrashing about as if knowing its only chance of survival was to break free. I cocked my head away and imagined a smooth squeeze of the trigger, something like you see in the movies. I pulled my finger, but nothing happened.

Clark's mouth began to move and I could hear words before he said them, "Damn City Slicker." "Man up, Guy." "Wimp." Tightening my grip, I pulled again, this time leveraging all the strength I could muscle in both hands. The shot rang out across the otherwise tranquil bay and ricocheted back again.

I glanced over at Clark and watched the corners of his eyes draw up, his bushy facial hair twitching. This was probably as close to a smile as I was going to see. I laid the pistol on the bench and hastily helped to get the lifeless fish into the boat. Boy's arms were completely in the water, his hands grabbing for the tail. The mouth of the fish was still held by the long-handled gaff in Clark's firm grasp. I went for the slimy fin below the gill and began pulling. The sixty pound test line was still connected to the hook which I assumed was deeply lodged somewhere inside the belly of the fish. I wondered if I should grab it, but decided to keep pulling on the fin. David stood back and watched, which was probably just as well.

With a few loud grunts and a lot of muscle power, the three of us hoisted the fish out of the water, securing its head on a hook near the top of the flag pole. I collapsed into the bench and watched the paper eagle fly tight circles above my catch. This fish was easily ten times bigger than any of the fish on the flyer, perhaps twenty times bigger than what I thought I'd catch. I reached for my pack and scavenged around for something to eat, feeling I'd more than earned it. Clark pulled a beer can from his cooler and Boy twisted the cap off a bottle of water. He laid a bottle on the bench next to me and took his first mate's seat beside Clark. Nobody said a word as we admired the prize between us. As I fed myself a handful of peanuts, my arms burning with fatigue, I saw David's eyes taking in the fish, then glancing over to me. "You did it Brother. You went halibut fishing in Alaska and you caught a really big fucking fish."

Blood trickled from the gunshot wound forming a small puddle on deck. I looked at Clark as he took a cigarette from the breast pocket of his flannel shirt and lit it without acknowledging my gaze.

"I reckon that fish weighs two hundred fifty pounds, give or take ten." A maniacal laugh erupted from his wrinkled lips. "Won't be good eating, but she's sure nice to look at. Biggest fish Little Hooker's seen, that's for damn sure."

"It's my first time fishing." I tried to hold back a little on the smile, since Clark was looking at me now. He tugged on his beard and laughed some more.

I looked back to David. He was pointing to the blood now thin and a washy shade of pink.

"Captain Clark, we seem to be taking on water." I tried not to sound alarmed. Clark took a long drag off his cigarette and shifted around in his seat. I heard the engine grind over a few times before it fired. Boy quietly pulled up anchor. I looked towards the early-summer, snow-capped mountains and then back at the fish again. Suddenly I felt dwarfed in our nineteen foot walk-around.

The engine cut out. Despite Clark's efforts to pump water from the boat, it was coming in faster. Something had to go. Clark rose from his chair and walked past me. He pulled the knife from his pocket and in one sweeping motion cut the fish free. It slithered to the deck with a body limp and its forgiving eyes cloudy-grey. The water was rising around our ankles now. I stood up and my feet slipped away. As I hit the deck I heard David yell, 'On your feet Brother, no regrets.'

Boy was desperately pulling life jackets from a box

under the bench while Clark grappled with the fish. I wrapped my legs around the bench, finding the best possible position, and we pushed the carcass overboard, my body stretching out over the railing. I let go and watched as my fish perched atop the water like a paper airplane before folding its wings and sinking into the sea. *Another senseless death.* Clark pulled me back into the boat and Boy thrust a life vest into my hands.

"Put it on!" Clark shouted, cracks showing in his cool captain facade. He pushed through the water and took a seat in the captain's chair. I watched him pull another gun from the cubby behind the steering wheel. He stood and fired a flare into the late afternoon sky. The water was nearly to my knees now. Protected by a thick, bright orange vest lashed to his chest, Boy opened the hinged window and struggled to pull himself up onto the high bow.

"Ferry'll be passin' through in about twenty minutes. Little Hooker's got a strong keel, she'll hold til then."

"This boat is sinking, keel or no keel," I shouted.

David looked at me, his eyes wondering what I was thinking. 'It's the sense of adventure, Brother, the thrill of passing very near the edge and wondering if your feet will find solid ground again.' I looked out across the water to the distant shoreline and then back to the boat again.

Clark and Boy were huddled in a tight embrace at the very tip of the bow. I could see they were shaking and Boy was crying. The sea, all around me now, was like a giant mirror reflecting my entire life back at me. David had one dream unrealized, one goal not yet achieved. *The things we do for love.*

I loosened the strap on my life vest and slipped over the railing. My body quickly submerged, my chest caving from the cold. Gasping for air, I started swimming for Land's End, swimming after David.

*

Cynthia Huijgens *After earning a BA in Art and Design and EdM in Art, Cynthia worked for many years in museum education. She is a graduate of The Writer's Studio, Simon Fraser University (SFU), Vancouver. An excerpt of her manuscript* The Novice Collector: Cosmic Strings and Ancient Things *appears in* Emerge 17, *SFU's annual anthology.*

Shyam Sunder Gopalakrishnan

Lily of the Valley

Pearls from the deepest seas,
for you I would gladly cede,
cause you drench me in glee,
only you I yearn to see,
so white and tender,
to your love I surrender,
as the autumn fell upon this valley,
you sang your divine melody,
Oh, Lily of the valley,
in lines I cannot write,
the way you mystify.

You shone bright,
like stars from the darkest nights,
your smiles like flowers,
borne of love and tears,
from the garden of Eden,
sent to me from heaven,

flowering in spring,
fragrance you bring,
Oh, Lily of the valley,
through clouds, along silver lines,
with you I wish to fly.

Oh, Lily of the valley,
in lines I cannot write,
the way you mystify.

I've Saved My Love for You

Like a red rose in June,
like a melody sung in tune,
you are special for me.
Like a youthful twilight,
like the silver moon light,
you shine to me.
I've saved my love for you,
I promise I'll keep it new.

Like a wild hurricane,
like a monsoon rain,
your love fell all over me.
Like a dark nightingale,
like a ship set sail,
don't drift from me.
'Cause I've saved my love for you,
I promise I'll keep it new.

Like an old Persian tale,
on my lost forlorn trail,
I came across you.
Through unseen tomorrows,
through grief and sorrow,
I'll be true to you.
Yes, I've saved my love for you,
and I promise I'll keep it new.

Silver Moon

Every evening as the sun goes down,
all I see is you rising, all alone,
through those clouds, in the darkness of the night,
my dear silver moon, may you shine your light.

Though lonesome you always seem to be,
though you hide behind clouds, from what I see,
though you wax and wane in your mother's arms,
you come up again with all your charms.

The waves rush to the shore at your behest,
but with every nightfall you shine without rest,
in the stillness of the night you ride through the
heavens,
and without your shining light, darkness descends.

Many a time, you've held me under your spell,
many a story, that I yearn to tell,
many a time, you've seen me dragged down,
many a dream, washed ashore from this town.

Though soon you'll be gone, may you shine,
upon everyone of us, on every hill we climb,
though at times you get red, though at times you get blue,
silver moon, silver moon, may your love shine through.

*

Shyam Sunder Gopalakrishnan is a post-doctoral researcher working in the field of hydrodynamics at the Université libre de Bruxelles (ULB). From a city named Cochin, on the south-west coast of India, he moved to Paris at the age of 21 to do his Masters at École Polytechnique. He is an ardent fan of P.G. Wodehouse, Albert Camus, Anton Chekhov, and Bob Dylan.

Antoinette Naomi Reddick

Sliding Memories

As JAZZ MUSIC WAFTS through the air outside the Sofitel Hotel New York, well dressed guests and patrons enter and exit. Most are all bundled up in tweed jackets and heavy overcoats, except for every now and then a minimally clad woman can be seen rushing from the valet to the lobby entryway. It's an obvious winter night because many are clutching their coats, to guard their body temperatures, while others are blowing into their palms attempting to bring warmth to their hands. Still, laughing and cheerful faces pretty much dominate the mood all around.

There is a certain high-society feel to this hotel because the valets and doorman are all dressed in classic tailored long tail tuxedos with accented bow ties. While each are wearing their best five-star smile, as they greet guests with the occasionally tipped hat. Absolutely, giving the impression that this is, indeed, an establishment for the elite.

Except for one oddly placed woman. A pretty, twenty something dishwater blonde, sobbing uncontrollably. She's outside, in the cold, near the hotel's entryway. Kneeling on the concrete, with both hands face down. Feverishly putting items, spilled onto the pavement, back inside her handbag, but no one's helping. What's also strange, no one is even taking a second glance. This young woman, who's clearly having a meltdown, is being completely ignored. She's wearing a silk nightgown and hotel slippers; perhaps she's a guest? Having a rather disturbing moment, to say the least, still, her behaviour doesn't seem to be enough to create concern. None of the service personnel, nor any of the guests going in and out of the hotel seem to mind. Except for this one exquisitely polished older woman, with ice white, perfectly-coiffed hair, dressed in black pants and a knitted black sweater accented with a Hermes belt. She's standing there watching, as she smokes a cigarette for a few moments while observing this frantic younger lady before deciding to intervene.

"Hello, are you okay?" The elderly lady inquires to the disheveled young woman. "Oh, you can see me?" The younger lady smirks, sarcastically.

"I know these New York personalities leave little to be desired in the considerate category," the older woman jests. "Let me help you."

The incredibly chic lady bends down gracefully while continuing to hold the cigarette between two fingers of her right hand, then gathers the scattered belongings and puts them back neatly into the woman's handbag.

"You see? It's all better now. I'm Eden," says the elegant mature woman as she wipes away the tears from the young lady's face. "All screws are fastened back into place. Nothing to worry about. See?" Eden gestures to the young woman as she offers the handbag with all of the recovered belongings. "What's your name? Eden inquires.

"Thanks. I'm Lyric." She says as she looks around, seeming a bit lost.

"Where are you going?" Eden probes.

"I don't know. I can't remember. I'm just confused, and I feel a little turned around. I... why am I telling you anything, I don't know you, leave me alone," Lyric balks.

Just like that, Lyric's tearful demeanor changes completely and her mood switches to closed and hostile. The next moment she storms off in a huff and walks down a busy Manhattan street toward Times Square. The sidewalk is filled with pedestrians so Lyric aggressively pushes her way through those impeding her pathway and continues to flit down the crowded street.

Eden, undeterred by Lyric's rudeness, looks up to the sky, slyly smiles, and mutters, "This is going to be an interesting night." Now following Lyric, Eden stays far enough behind her to keep out of sight, but close enough to maintain Lyric's whereabouts. She leisurely walks and smokes, just casually walking and smoking, while Lyric hurries down the boulevard, nervously rushing out in front of speeding cars, attempting to hail any taxi driving by. Until Lyric's had enough of her own self and breaks down once again. Only this time, it's in the middle of a crowded Times Square.

She again begins to bawl like a child throwing a tantrum, appearing more helpless than before.

Looking aimlessly, she says, "Why won't anybody help me? Why won't the cabs stop for me? I just want to go home," Lyric protests as Eden quickly moves in to assist her.

"I'm helping you," Eden insists as she picks Lyric up by both arms, from the side of the roadway, and quickly flags down a taxi. Lyric reluctantly gets inside, then Eden hops in after her.

"Why are you following me?" Lyric huffs.

"I'm not following you, I'm helping you," Eden replies.

"Then why are you helping me? I didn't ask for your help."

"Weren't you just screaming for help back there?" Eden insists.

A defeated Lyric relents and lets this soft, elegant stranger take the lead.

"Which way you headed?" Demands a raspy voice, coming from the driver in the front seat.

"Will you just pull over to the side of the road for a

moment, please? I'll tell you in a minute," Eden replies.

"I want to go home," Lyric anxiously interjects.

"Ok, where is home?" Eden gently prods.

"I don't remember. I've been looking for a while, but I seem to have forgotten. I can't remember anything," Lyric responds, expressing more confusion.

"What's the last thing you can remember?" asks Eden.

"I don't know. It's fuzzy. Maybe it's because I'm hungry and can't think straight," Lyric says.

"How about this, we get you something to eat and then we'll see if we can find your home. Deal?"

Lyric shrugs her shoulders as Eden instructs the taxi driver to take them to the restaurant Serendipity.

It's a typical late Saturday night in New York. Drunkards are celebrating amongst themselves, laughing boisterously along the bustling city's sidewalks. As Eden assists Lyric into Serendipity, a spot that seems rather lively for this late-night hour.

They are both seated at a round table in the middle of a mystical wonderland themed restaurant. Set in front of them are two big goblets filled with syrupy thick hot cocoa, mounds of whipped cream and chunks of shaved chocolate, accompanied by a hot plate of French fries. It was the only thing on the menu that Lyric could remember the taste of. Everything else just seemed to throw her back into a confused state. So, to avoid getting riled up again, she settled for good ole fashioned fries. Eden and Lyric, spending a good bulk of time over their hot cocoa, keep the discussions on anything that would jar her memory and help her come out of this lost and confused state. Nothing is helping, until Eden says, "there you go, better now? Fit as a fiddle?" Lyric, wide-eyed and curious, explains how her grandmother used to always say that to her, every time she tucked her into bed during summer visits.

Suddenly, the surroundings begin to change. Eden and Lyric find themselves in a wheat field, on a warm sunny day. The wind is gently blowing a tall patch of wheat, in one direction. Making the sound leaves make as they brush against each other, in the wind. The field is like a moving painting with golden hues of yellow, toasted browns and juniper greens. The breeze is warm and the mood tranquil. Set just beyond the field, is a white house, Victorian in appearance, with black window panes and a brick red door.

"Nana's house!" Lyric exclaims. "I used to spend every summer here as a child. Wait a minute? What's going on? How did we get here? Am I dreaming?"

Eden tells Lyric to not be alarmed, that she has brought them here hoping it will help her to remember. She explains it's a special gift that she has and only uses it when she feels it's necessary to help others remember.

"Are you a sorceress?" A startled Lyric spits out.

"No, I'm nothing of the sort," Eden chuckles. "Please calm yourself, I'm just trying to help you remember so that you can go home. Don't you want to go home?"

As Lyric nods yes, the two of them begin to walk through the red unlocked door into a cozy country home. The closer they get to the living room, the more apparent the sounds become. Feet are tapping against a hardwood floor, and an off-key piano is playing. The sounds mimic someone slowly trying to piece together *Twinkle Twinkle Little Star*.

As they enter the great room, a dark-haired man, who looks of Native American descent is sitting on a tattered chestnut brown sofa. His legs are outstretched, as one bare foot casually crosses the other. He is reading the *Sunday Gazette*. The sun is lightly peeking in through the multi-paned door that leads out to the back yard. A little girl in a baby blue dress with a pink ribbon fastened at the back is skipping in circles, around the sofa, where the man is contentedly sitting. In the same room, a little boy about 6 years old is seated at a black shiny piano, banging away on the keys. The little girl, who appears to also be 5 or 6 years old, is singing.

"Ring around the rosie, a pocketful of posies. Ashes! Ashes! We all fall down." Just as the little girl says down, she collapses and sits on the floor. The old man looks up from his newspaper and smiles at the little girl playing.

Her playful singing goes on for several minutes until a voice calls out from another room.

"Lyri!" The voice demands. Unfazed, the little girl

keeps singing her song and dropping like a swatted fly every time the song ends.

"Lyri!" An elderly lady appearing to be in her seventies sticks her head out from the kitchen. "Lyri, come on now and help your nana get lunch ready." Water begins to well in Lyric's eyes.

"I remember this day," Lyric says as she wipes away the tears that have begun to stream down her face. "This is the day my grandmother died. "Why did you bring me here? This isn't helping me."

Eden, not bothered by any of the upset, coaxes Lyric to pay closer attention and to think about what she could remember from this moment.

Everything seemed to move in slow motion for Lyric. From little Lyri playing to her running toward the kitchen to help her grandmother.

"Now, what do you remember about this moment?" Eden asks again.

Coming out of the daze these images were throwing her into, Lyric answers.

"I remember how happy I was. How Nana and Grampy were my two favourite people in the world. How they both died that summer and me and my twin brother, Laryd, never played as freely as we did during those summers ever again. My mom was always pushing us to work so hard. Me with my singing and my brother with his piano playing. She was relentless."

At the word relentless, a new scene emerges. A finely kempt Park Avenue penthouse appears. This time, instead of the peaceful country images from before, everything is austere and sterile, with the exception of pop music being played on the piano. It's the song, *Papa Don't Preach* by Madonna. A little girl is singing, a young boy is playing the music and a woman with olive-toned skin is directing them.

"Ha!" Shrieking from disgust. "This was me and my brother rehearsing for our first competition. I believe we were 8 years old and she had me singing this silly song. Can you believe a grown woman making two little children perform, *Papa Don't Preach*? She wanted me to be a big star, just like Madonna."

Eden remains quiet.

"You see that ruler in her hand?" Lyric continues. Wait for it... There! See there; she just hit me on the back of my head with it! If either my brother or I made a mistake, we'd get swatted with that stick, every time. She was such a ruthless witch."

"Why do you think your memories brought us here? Eden asks.

"I don't have a clue. Maybe it's because I hated singing and it was something my mother forced me to do. I was terrified of that ruler, and I just wanted to please her, so I went along with it. This was also the only way I could get her to pay attention to me. Any attention is better than no attention, right?" Lyric responds.

"Yes, but why this moment Lyric? We are not moving. Your energy wants us to know something more about this experience," Eden persists.

"Ummm, well, I became really good at it, my singing, and I realised that if I just made my mom happy, then she'd love me. So I kept going along with what she wanted."

Another memory emerges. This time it's backstage in the left wing of a huge theatre. The audience is full and a teenage girl with blonde hair, wearing a skimpy red dress and a full face of makeup, stands nervously looking out onto the empty stage. Straightening the girl's hair and outfit is the same olive-toned woman from the Park Avenue apartment. This time her voice can be heard.

"Remember, what's the motto? The woman asks with a slight southern drawl.

"Make mama proud." The teenager recites.

Eden and Lyric are standing just behind the girl and her mother.

"This was when I was 15 years old. By this time, it was maybe my 30th competition, but I was still scared to death!" Lyric chuckles as she continues to explain. "These things were always so absurd to me. At this point, I wasn't even nervous anymore about singing, but I was always so petrified about disappointing mother. If I lost or even came in second place, oh gosh, you could forget about it; she wouldn't talk to me for days. Then, once she did start talking to me, I'd never hear the end of it. She'd yell at me and berate me for weeks."

Then I'd be forced to train even harder for the next competition or performance. It was a vicious cycle of her being either cold to me or pushing me, but never just loving me."

Lyric continues to explain to Eden about how the hounding efforts of her mother only stopped when Lyric landed her first singing contract with Sony records. She shares how she went on to open for big acts like Sade and Britney Spears. And talks about how her mother's pushiness later stopped, but quickly switched to boasting about her instead. Lyric then shivers at the recollection of these memories and begins to describe how her mother's bragging affected her.

"That's when the anxiety turned from fear of losing my mother's love to fear of falling out of the limelight."

Lyric then goes on to list countless stories about how she hated her mom and singing. She reflects on how trapped and isolated she felt growing up.

Just as she remembers her feelings of loneliness, Lyric is taken to another memory. It's a huge theatre, and a sexily-dressed Lyric is getting ready to hit the stage. Behind the curtain and off to the side of the stage, Lyric and a handsome man in his late 40's, with caramel skin and a muscular build, are kissing passionately. His hands are up her dress, and one of her legs is wrapped around his waist. Soft moans can be heard.

"Oh," Lyric mutters, covering her mouth in

embarrassment, "Kenny, my manager. This is a big event. All of the big wigs are in the audience, and I'm about to hop on stage to do a set. This night, we're testing some new music for global distribution. This was the moment he asked me to marry him and promised me that we would be together forever. Just me and him. I didn't have to be alone anymore. It would no longer be only about the music; I had someone who genuinely cared about me. This night I was so excited about going on stage and singing my heart out."

That's when the two stop passionately making out, an ecstatic Lyric checks her makeup and hair in a mirror then rushes off to greet an eager sold out audience. The two of them, both Eden and Lyric, listen to the beautiful sounds of Lyric's voice as she sings the songs from her new album.

"You have a beautiful voice," Eden remarks.

"Thank you."

She is smiling and seems to light up the stage with her presence during every song. Finishing to a standing ovation, and beaming from ear to ear. An excited Lyric exits the stage looking like she's on top of the world, only to discover Kenny standing arm and arm, next to a sophisticated woman in her early 40's. The expression on both Lyrics' faces change from glee to disappointment.

"What's going on here?" Eden asks.

"It's his wife." Lyric responds. "He had been lying to

me for months. He told me that he'd left her and that night she showed up looking for him. She said that she was there to support me. Look at her; she looks at least five months pregnant! He's such a liar and a user. It turns out he was using me, just like my mom and everyone else. He was never serious about being with me." Lyric's voice begins to quiver, and she soon starts to cry. "My singing was like a sentence until I met him, but this moment I realised nothing had changed."

"What do you mean, nothing had changed?" Eden asks.

"I mean, that was the moment I realised this world was not for me. There's no happiness in it, only lies and people using me for their gain. This is the moment when I decided I'd be better off dead." Lyric says with resignation.

Sirens can be heard faintly in the distance and Lyric begins to become lightheaded and woozy, starting to stumble over a bit. That's when they find themselves back at the Sofitel hotel, this time though, they are not outside, but in a penthouse suite. There's complete pandemonium all around because the paramedics are giving mouth-to-mouth resuscitation to a woman lying lifeless on the hotel room floor.

Eden and Lyric are standing amongst the chaos of a room packed with emergency workers and hotel staff rushing in and out. This is when Eden tells Lyric her true identity:

"I am the Guardian of Death, here to take you home,

Lyric. The home you've been searching for all night is the afterlife and I'm here to usher you there."

She then continues to explain to Lyric that the reason why she had been so foggy all night, was because she had taken a lot of pills in an attempt to kill herself and those pills were going to take her life, this very night. In just a little while. And that she is there to grant her desire to die and to take the pain away and help her escape all the suffering, permanently.

This is a moment of truth for Lyric because she is now face to face with death. Life, as she's known it, has come to an end and the only thing she can feel is shock. Then, in an instant, like the raging waters of Niagara Falls, all of the pain from her life of isolation and feeling trapped, in someone else's story, begins to rush in and Lyric collapses on the floor in agony.

Eden continues to explain to her that if she wanted, she could die this night and that all of that pain would be taken away in a matter of moments; however, that there is also another option, one where Lyric could stay. She could go back and deal with her life. Face all of the misery, that was suddenly becoming more and more noticeable, head on and find a way to make peace with things. Or she could choose to leave the pain behind, where that lifeless body lay.

But, if she did choose to die, then she would be forced to repeat the same cycle again until she could beat this pain and move beyond it, once and for all.

"You see Lyric, you have only about two minutes to

decide before they stop performing CPR on you and pronounce you dead. So what will it be? Are you going to come with me or are you going to stay and find your own place in life and redefine what it means to you to be alive?

What's it going to be?"

For one brief moment, Lyric pauses, then winces her face and grabs her chest and says the words,

"I can't..."

In that instant, it was as if time sped up and there was nothing but light followed by a gasp of breath. Sounds of coughing and gagging can be heard, coming from the now slowly moving body on the penthouse suite floor. Lyric had made her choice, and it was a courageous one. She was ready to find her own piece of home, no pressure, no rules, just her heart and her desires. Those last words spoken to Eden were:

"I can't leave life, not this way."

*

Antoinette Naomi Reddick is a Master trainer of various schools of thought, trainer of NLP, writer, business and empathic spiritual life coach whose passion is neo-anthropology, the study of human behaviour from a modern perspective. After spending three years traveling the world and observing human culture, Antoinette uses her creative writing with the intention of inspiring, uplifting and transforming others.

Richard Boland

Above and Beyond All Reason

Heath,
with whom I sang together in the Gay Men's Choir. He'd steal glances, eying me from across the bass section and I couldn't help but smile. He looked fine. One day Heath did not show up. Someone told me in the elevator at Portland State University, where we rehearsed Monday nights. 'He's positive.' In the eighties this word developed another, opposite meaning. I never saw him again.

Gerald,
who composed music. I still know how to pound out one of his musical phrases on the piano and I think of him every time I play it. Gerry, who refused to cut his afro, even though his hair had receded. I don't think he ever wanted to give up disco. I saw him dance up a sweat at the 'Family Zoo' on the gay strip on SW Oak Street, where they served acid punch. I read his obituary in the *Daily Oregonian*.

Matthew,

who told nobody. We called him 'Matchou', like his Filipino friend did. His laugh was sweet and contagious. I found a picture of him standing naked in tall grass, lying around on Andy's dining room table. Andy had taken it years ago on Sauvie Island. They had taken one picture each, for each other. But Matthew's right to privacy no longer mattered. He'd suddenly gone home to live with his parents back in Idaho, where he spent the last few months of his life.

Ted,

who gave away his belongings while he was still alive. We sat in his living room on SW Vista Avenue, and he asked me what I wanted. Out the window, an entire wooded hillside was scraped off to make way for a level parking lot. I told him to hold on to all of it, but he insisted I take something. He slipped off his bow tie and taught me how to knot it. He was buried in another one.

Geofrey,

whom I last saw at Good Samaritan Hospital, all wired up, a respirator mask covering his nose and mouth. He could not talk. I remember his blue eyes. They were the same. The rest of his face I hardly recognized. I held his hand, listened to the beeps of the monitors, and his laborious breathing. Dale, his lover, lost most of their belongings when the family stopped by after the funeral. They claimed it as legal inheritance.

Tim,

who wrote musicals, zillions of them. His drag queen name was Eileen Over. I saw him perform in one of his own musicals at the City Grill on the 30th floor of the Big Pink, the US Bank tower. He'd left the large price tag on his dress, maybe so he could return it the next day. His brain got effected eventually. Dementia. His boyfriend Max took care of him as long as he could, until Tim's intelligence was too far gone. He was moved to hospice care on SE 60th and Alder Street. Max visited him daily to the last day.

Marc,

who was Rainbow's daddy, the Springer Spaniel who always took the front seat in the car, right next to him. We hiked in the Columbia Gorge together, in the rain, his dog on our heels. Soft spoken Marc, he showed me his first spot on his chest. Kaposi's sarcoma. He told me about his favorite place in the world near Manzaneta on the Pacific coast. His doctor cried at his bedside. His ashes were put in the ocean wind on top of Ne-ah-kah-nie mountain, just like he wanted.

Vince,

who was my neighbor, Horace's love. He lost his job as a kindergarten teacher. He was fired. Then Vince went blind and lost his ability to walk. I remember we carried him up the steps to have dinner with us. Horace explained, so he knew which food was where on the dinner plate. Salad at nine o' clock, pasta at three. Horace mourned for years. He wrote a play about the process and performed it in our friend Catherine's apartment on SE Grand Avenue. 'Talking in the dark...without you.'

Harold,
with whom I danced in 'Oklahoma!', the musical. 'Once you go black you don't go back,' he told me. At the church funeral in Clatskenie, rural Oregon, we found the small group of his friends, all of us apart from his conservative Christian family. In the order of service, it read he had died of complications of pneumonia, because that sounded cleaner in Clatskenie.

Happy go lucky Michael,
who built huge, fantastic sandcastles on the beach. He and Joel made love one Sunday morning on the floor of their downtown apartment, while they thought I was asleep in the loft. The noises woke me up. Michael had just been accepted into medical school. He was taken into emergency and was gone in three weeks. His lover Joel never got over it. This large man cried and cried with no tears left and not a soul on this earth knew how to comfort him.

Fredrick,

who'd married his lover Randall, decades before their commitment was considered legal. A priest in the garden, a wedding cake, exchange of rings, the whole nine yards. The last time I visited Fred was at their house, Randall and Fred's SE Portland home. He was hooked up on medication three hours every day. He wanted to die in his own home and not in the hospital. He did.

Randall,

Fredrick's husband, who worked out at the same gym as I did. The lawyer, who dressed in crisp white shirts and wore expensive leather-soled shoes. He got thinner and thinner. His arms, his body, his face. Only his large brown eyes became larger. He fed, kissed, washed, held, laughed with, cried with, slept with Fred and finally outlived him by three weeks.

Roger,

who lived out in the country, with Tomas. Roger, who was a Lutheran priest, taught me to ski in the wooded hills around the vicarage. One crisp Saturday morning, we sat at the breakfast table, reminiscing about Tomas, who'd passed away some months before. Roger seemed at peace. He believed in heaven. Their separation would be temporary. Five years after he had followed Tomas, the cathedral filled with 2500 people. It was the venue for a photo exhibition 'Ecce homo', depicting Jesus among homosexuals. The cathedral's Dean recognized Roger, by calling the art event a tribute to him.

Jesse,

whose brother bought the house on NW Northrup Street in which he rented a room, just so he could stay and live there until the end. Jesse, who'd had three-somes, who enjoyed life. Who played cowboy and drove a Range Rover with a spare tire on the back that read 'Rodeo'. His friends made him a quilt after he died. I found it by surprise when the memorial AIDS quilt covered the entire National Mall in Washington DC.

Daniel,

whose partner, Nathan, took a small group of friends to a meadow filled with blue gentians in the Mount Hood wilderness, a year to the day Daniel had died. The sun shone brightly, lighting up the snow-covered mountain peak above the timberline. Nathan opened the small cardboard box, and we took turns spreading Dan's ashes on the grass. When we looked up, two deer passed by. It could not have been more perfect.

I,

who became the coincidental survivor, eventually was at loss to live. Simply too much loss of life. Connections severed. Futures disappeared, forever. With each of my friends, I buried my grief, my passion to love intimately, my courage to live. Overly protective, locked up by fear, I retreated deep inside me. How else could I escape death?

I,
who found himself in a solitary place, clinging too long to lonely relationships. As if my life depended on it. And, it did. The bottle empty, the mind full of skeletons, I froze, and let the snow cover me. Life a total white out, black out. Numb. Cold. Still. Until finally, at long last, I whispered: "Help me." To utter these two words was most difficult to do.

All of them
answered my call. One by one, I dug them up. I let go of the pain, the guilt, the sorrow. I had to. But I kept the love. With all of them secured in my memory, love did survive.

Love,
vulnerable, beautiful, comforting love. Risky love. It will still be there when I'm gone. Above and beyond all reason.

*

Richard Maria Boland. A native of the Netherlands, Richard lived in Sweden and in Oregon, USA, before settling in Belgium. He wrote his first novel, Noble, The Secret of The Sacred Mountain, a coming-of-age story of an eleven-year-old boy, published in 2015.

Sarah Strange

Saved by the Bell!

That Belgium is surreal is a well-known fact
It doesn't take one long to cotton on to that!
I often gasp with wonder when it's bin man day
To see the little treasures that Belgians throw away.

All sorts of things are jettisoned—sometimes not in
   bags
Sports gear past its best; a broken chair that sags
The owners hope these pre-loved goods will vanish out
   of sight
So no trace will be found when they return at night.

Today I strolled in vacant mood down my local street
And came across a doll's house, brightly painted, clean
   and neat
How sad to see it lying there, unloved and rejected
Soon the cart will rumble past, and it will be collected.

It seems too good to throw away, and toys do not
   come cheap

I consider its predicament—such wastage; I could
  weep
And then the local school bell rings, the kids all rush
  outside
A mini, laughing cohort; will this mansion be espied?

As if in answer to my prayer, one child runs up the
  slope;
And crouches down beside it, so my heart beats with
  new hope.
A parent follows suit, so this tenancy is filled
A rescue is effected, and a little girl is thrilled.

A Word on Language

English idioms are fun:
Ever seen anyone "jump the gun"?
How do butterflies reach your tum?
It's quite absurd;
And can a person be "bad news"?
What's an offer "you can't refuse"?
What happens when you "pay your dues"?
What's in a word?

There's "feeling blue" and "seeing red"
"Green" fingers in the flowerbed
A "brown study" is somewhere else instead
It makes no sense;
Figures of speech—a wealthy store
The English love a metaphor,
A practice foreigners deplore
Things get intense!

So much is just implied—not said
"Up the garden path" we're led
"End of the day", does not mean bed;
Brits stand apart;
Universal language? I'm not sure
Vocab-rich, weird grammar lore
Yet children have this knack at four
They learn by heart.

A Tribute to Leonard Cohen

He sang of solitude and sex
Relationships fraught and complex
With a warm faith that touched our heart
Leonard—why did you have to part?

Poems and songs of deep malaise
Reflecting youth's tumultuous days
His Sixties' "Suzanne" by the river
In many of us sends a shiver ...

Folk music, cabaret and stage
On the Isle of Wight with Hendrix plays
His gravelly voice will haunt our dreams
His words have tapped into deep seams.

Subconsciously we hear him still
He caught our mood, morose or thrill
Modest, unassuming, kind
His trademark black hat was a blind

His face in shadow so we heard
And tuned into each poignant word
Montreal claims him for their own
His sudden death means we're alone.

Finger-on-the-pulse through six decades
Leonard Cohen's music never fades
His passing cuts me like a knife...
Hallelujah for his life!

*

Sarah Strange finds poetic inspiration in nature, people, life events, current affairs, emotions, the quirky side of life... She self-published A Turn in the Road, an anthology of a bereavement, in 2014. Her next book will be about Brussels, her home since 1973 where she is a qualified tourist guide. www.poetinthewoods.blogspot.com

Ross Noble

Homecoming

'Homecoming' is the opening chapter of the novel The Wisher *about a very special teenage boy called Beau who is struggling with bullying. After moving in with their dad for a fresh start, Beau and his twin sister Blanca soon discover they are witches and have to act fast to learn how their powers work and where they came from. Things become even more complicated when Beau falls in love with Christian Sutherland, the mysterious and reviled local heart-throb with plenty of secrets of his own.*

WORST IDEA EVER. Without a doubt! If there were a world record for worst idea, this would qualify. Why on Earth had I let my know-it-all sister talk me into this move in the first place?

The coin slipped from my hand and hit the water—*plunk*—, sinking steadily to the bottom of the fountain with the countless others. I squeezed my eyes tightly shut to block out the bustling medieval *plaza* around me and laced my fingers together to make a wish. But it wasn't as easy as it used to be when all I wanted was a new bike, extra pocket money or some other trifle. Now I wasn't wishing for any *thing*, just a change of direction. For things to look up at last.

"*¡Por favor!*" I mumbled, wringing my hands until they went white at the knuckles. "*¡Por favor!*"

Standing in shorts and T-shirt under the August sun, Barcelona must have seemed like heaven to the hordes of tourists, and yet to me it had become hell. All because of them: the bullies I couldn't shake.

A fist flew through my memories. It slammed into my jaw and sent me crashing to the hard, cobbled, floor. Not these cobbles in this square, but far across town. At school.

Instinctively, I winced, my body cowering away a fraction to shield itself before the next remembered blow could fall in my mind. As it must. As it always did when these black thoughts broke through. I hated these memories, hated that they were part of me now. They stung, like a raw wound, leaving a quaking in my chest and a weakness in my knees. Worse than the real bullies, the memories followed me everywhere, lying in wait around dark corners when I was out with friends or at the beach with my sister.

Worse still, they had invaded my home, hiding under the bed and in the closet to wake me shaking and screaming in the dead of night. It was a new low. I wasn't tough by nature, but I'd never felt so small or helpless before. All I wanted was to curl up into a ball and cry all the time. My reaction was as humiliating to me as the bullying itself.

"*¡Por favor!*" I sniffed and used the back of my hand to wipe away a stupid tear, one of far too many since this all began. "I don't know what I'll do if..."

I couldn't finish the sentence. I realised only too well where it led. That's why I had to go.

A breeze trickled in under the arches of the stiflingly hot stone *plaza,* and I opened my eyes at last for one final glimpse of the fountain. Yes, totally the worst idea ever, but what choice did I have?

"It'll be raining, of course," Mum called when she heard the apartment door close behind me. "It rains all the time in Scotland!"

"I know, Mum!" I called back, resting my head against the doorframe for a moment to collect my thoughts and hide the chinks in my resolve. "You already said. About a million times," I added under my breath.

At least I could say I wasn't the first Harris to run away from his problems: fleeing was in the family. After a boring, rain-soaked childhood in Scotland—her words, not mine—Mum had fallen pregnant and married too young. Way too young! Feeling trapped, she did the only thing she could: without telling a soul, she caught a train with her newborns and didn't stop until Spain.

It caused a huge family rift. You should have heard the rows whenever Gran, Aunt Ella and Bobby came to visit. But Mum was stubborn and, in the end, cut all ties. She practically forbid any questions about family or her old home. Only Dad still visited with Bobby in tow each summer. Being forbidden made the Highlands seem mysterious and fascinating to us as kids. I guess that's why I was so apprehensive about moving there now. I still couldn't quite believe she was actually letting us go at all. But then, lemon-sized bruises change everything, don't they?

"Mum! There's a weight limit, stop!" I pleaded when I found her in my little bedroom at the back of our apartment, compulsively cramming things into my already bulging suitcase. I pulled the latest additions—last summer's favourite shorts and a flimsy T-shirt I'd barely worn—back out and gawked. "I can't even wear this stuff in Oban."

She turned away and busied herself smoothing imagined wrinkles from the yellow blanket on my twin sister's already empty bed. "Beau, listen," she said with a serious frown, "we should talk—"

"Mum, please!" I interrupted before she repeated the same objections I'd heard too often these last few weeks. "I need a fresh start like we said." Taking her small hands in mine and sitting us on my bed, I pleaded with my eyes for her not to make this any harder than it already was. "Besides," I added, "Blanca's already there now. She's expecting me."

Her shoulders dropped in defeat, and we were both silent. She'd never have given up that easily before, but she wasn't her old self anymore. I'd watched the worry eat away at her in recent months, etching lines into her brow and multiplying the grey in her otherwise glorious red hair. She was thinner—too thin—and her eyes were puffy and laden with heavy purple bags from the sleepless nights she thought I didn't know about. It was all my fault; I had to stay strong now, for both our sakes.

I squeezed her hands a little tighter, rubbing my thumbs over her knuckles and at last she responded. "Okay." Her voice quavered with repressed emotion. She pulled her hands free and blotted her eyes, nodding. "Okay," she said again more firmly. "But you're not leaving without this."

From under my pillow, she pulled a brown paper parcel tied with some ribbon I recognised from her sewing basket. "I know it's not your fountain," she apologised, a mischievous twinkle in her eye. "But there's a weight limit."

I smiled and exhaled in relief at her joke because it was so typical of her. You see, the thing you have to understand about my Mum is that she *knows* me. Sometimes better than I know myself. So I wasn't surprised she knew where I'd spent my last day in town, just like I shouldn't have been surprised when, at thirteen, after several agonising months building up my courage, I came out to her, and she just smiled and said, "Of course, dear. I've always known, it just shines out of you."

It was a relief, really, once I got over the shock. Though it did make me a little self-conscious... ok, a lot self-conscious. I basically spent the next six months sitting on my hands at school just in case they were too flouncy. And we're talking *Spain* here! They're all flouncy with their hands!

"I bet half the coins in that old fountain are yours," she said quietly, watching me tug open the ribbon and part the folds of tissue paper beneath. Inside was a homemade dreamcatcher decorated with shells and beads, dappled grey and blond feathers and even a tiny rainbow flag. "You've always loved it. Ever since I took you two there as kids and you pretended it was a wishing well."

"Mum, I..." My voice choked in my rapidly swelling throat.

Reading me perfectly, as always, she reached out and cupped my cheek. "If anyone deserves to have his wishes come true, it's you, my sweet boy." Heavy tears trembled on my eyelids, but she brushed them away quickly. "Promise you'll hang it the moment you get there?" I threw my arms around her neck and nodded into her shoulder. "And promise you'll be careful? You have no idea—"

"Of course, Mum!" I cleared my throat and stood to stem the impending tsunami of maternal *angst*. "I promise."

I slipped the dreamcatcher carefully between two brand new, Scotland-proof jumpers and zipped the case shut with a sense of finality. "There," I said, taking one last look around the only bedroom I'd ever known. "It's getting late, let's go."

*

Dad met me in the busy arrivals lounge with a woolly jumper in one hand and an irritated look on his face. He was a tall man (genes I hadn't inherited) with a pale complexion and auburn hair (I got both of those) and was best described as the 'strong silent type'. I had no idea what Mum ever saw in him; they were chalk and cheese.

"Good flight?" he asked, holding out the jumper and taking the too-heavy case I was struggling with.

"Fine. Nothing to report," I said, taking a closer look at the misshapen, beige monster now in my hands.

"Right," he nodded, "get that on. You're late."

He pointed towards the exit and the carpark beyond and strode off, me trailing at his heels. I felt the drop in temperature the minute we stepped outside the terminal. "No going back now," I mumbled to myself, pulling the insanely too-large jumper over my head and pushing the sleeves up until my hands finally reemerged.

"Hurry up, Robert!" he shouted, using my full first name and looking back over his shoulder, clearly annoyed. "It's extra after ten minutes."

Dad reached the car first, parked at the far end of the multi-story carpark, in a section intended for quick drop-offs. He unlocked the boot, lifted my over-stuffed suitcase with both hands, and wrestled with it for several minutes to make it fit atop the tools and other bits and pieces he kept back there. He shook his head at it and me for overpacking. While I waited, I couldn't help but check the backseat just in case, but, as I suspected, she wasn't there. I had a lot of bridges to mend. Starting now.

"She's at home," Dad said, at last, giving up on the boot. He shoved my case in the back seat and slammed the door behind it. "Get in!"

We didn't talk much during the drive, the awkward silence only occasionally punctuated by Dad's sporadic commentary of the sights along the way. Both of us carefully avoided what was really on our minds: gay son, bullied, fleeing.

That suited me fine. The whole situation was so tense and uncomfortable; it had me screwing my hands together nervously in my lap for the first twenty miles or so. Plus, there would be plenty of time to talk later. Or maybe we could avoid it altogether and pretend nothing had ever happened.

Either way, as we left the airport and then the motorway far behind, and pushed deep into the countryside, it suddenly hit me: I was actually here, in Scotland, at last. After so many nights in bed as a kid dreaming about this moment; after bugging Bobby with hundreds of questions on his visits—he was the only one who would flout Mum's edict—and after even scheming to run away here with my sister when we both turned eighteen or after university or something: I was actually here. All I wanted was to sit quietly and watch it all whizzing by through the windscreen. Even if the sky was an unrelenting grey. Even if it was raining cats and dogs in August. Even if the circumstances couldn't have been worse. I was actually here.

About an hour into the drive I stole a glance at Dad out of the corner of my eye just as he did the same, pity and confusion written across his face. I folded my arms over my chest and turned away quickly, trying very hard to focus on the scenery, but suddenly the landscape wasn't so interesting anymore.

I wished I hadn't made such a mess, hadn't kept so many secrets for so long. That was my big mistake. None of them got it. To me, the bullying wasn't real as long as no one knew. But there was nothing I could do when, in June, just a few weeks after my fifteenth birthday, they found me curled up in bed with a black eye and dried blood smeared across my face. My shirt was torn, and I couldn't stop shaking or even form a coherent sentence.

My mum and twin sister rallied round, holding me in shifts for hours until, finally, I was able to cough up the truth. Then Mum called Dad. "He needs to know," she insisted, and "might know what to do." She didn't realise he had no idea.

Dad knew exactly what to do: he slammed the 'phone down. For a man that almost never displayed any emotion, I got the message loud and clear.

Mum was furious. She called him right back and kept trying until he took her call. He apologised eventually, claiming shock. Whatever. I blamed myself more than him. We hadn't talked since, until today.

Things with Blanca weren't the same anymore either. We had always been close before, inseparable, told one another everything. But not about the bullying. I just felt so ashamed, as if they could see something in me that deserved to be punished. How could I tell anyone about that?

Whatever the reasons, my sister was pissed. Pissed at the bullies and especially pissed at me. She resented my shutting her out like I'd broken some unwritten twin rule or something. We were barely talking. That's the only reason I agreed to her stupid idea of moving here at all: to make it up to her. Deep down, I knew she was exploiting my situation as a pretext to get to Scotland, using me in a way. But I didn't know what else to do. Besides, I never imagined Mum would agree to it!

God! I thought, squeezing my chest even tighter and stealing another glance at Dad. Bee was right, as usual. The telephone was definitely the wrong way to break the news to him. I was lucky he was letting me move in at all.

I sank down deeper into my seat and went over everything again in my head, for the umpteenth time, promising myself things would be different now. I'd make it up to them all. I'd fit in this time, and I'd keep my damn mouth shut about you-know-what.

"There," Dad said gruffly, rousing me from my thoughts. He pointed straight ahead and, just over the crest of yet another hill, Oban came into view below. It was no more than a handful of old stone houses and other buildings huddled around a small bay, just exactly as tiny as Mum had always complained, yet far more beautiful and picturesque than I had expected. It made me smile at once.

Dad's place was a different matter. I'm not sure how I envisaged his house, but from the let-down feeling in the pit of my stomach when we pulled up outside barely five minutes later, I figured this wasn't it.

An adorable little cottage or one of the fine, grand buildings down by the bay it wasn't. Instead, it was a grey semi at the end of a row of identical, post-war buildings. And it had certainly seen better days: the green paintwork on the door and gate desperately needed to be re-done; all around it, untended grass grew like shabby fuzz on a forgotten tomato; and every one of the paving slabs was either split, out of place, or wobbled underfoot as Dad trundled my case up to the front door.

Inside it was small and outdated but not bad. To the left was a living room and behind it, just past the loo under the stairs, the kitchen-diner.

"This way," he pointed and turned sideways so his broad shoulders and my case would fit up the narrow staircase just inside the front hall.

At the top of the landing were the bedrooms: the master at the back and our room at the front with the only bathroom sandwiched in between. Blanca and I were sharing, just like at home.

"Right," he said, pushing the bedroom door open. He swung the case in the air, and it landed, bouncing on the bed. "What do you think?"

It was a small, square room with a large window overlooking the front garden. The walls were off-white, the carpet blue. On one side there was a wardrobe, small desk and chair, and on the other a lamp, bookshelf and bed. Just one bed.

"What's going on?" I asked, totally puzzled. "Where's Blanca's stuff?"

"Well now," Dad began to explain, rubbing his big, dry hands. "That's my wee surprise. I've done a little work to the house."

"Huh? You're not really the D.I.Y. type, Dad!" I said accusingly, thinking of the garden outside and remembering past disasters in Barcelona.

"Well, uh." He looked a little offended but cleared his throat and ploughed on. "You'll be staying here. Your sister's got the extension out back."

I was stunned. No, I was more than stunned! My own room? "Wow, Dad. That's..." I couldn't find the right word. I looked all around, taking it in again. It seemed so much bigger, huge even, now I didn't have to share it. At last, I turned back to him, smiled and just settled for, "Thank you."

"Ach, you're welcome," he mumbled. "I want you to be happy here."

I nodded in agreement. Dad didn't do emotions, so that was big for him. And this was a big gesture.

"Seriously, Dad," I said sincerely. "Thanks. It will be nice to have some privacy."

His brow furrowed. "Yes, privacy, but that doesn't mean…" He cleared his throat again. "Well, there are house rules, you know!" He didn't say the words, but it was obvious he meant 'no boys'.

I was shocked and annoyed, mostly because I suspected he'd have rejoiced at me bringing a girl home. But, before I could object, he turned and left, the floorboards of the stairs creaking under his bulk on his way back down.

Blanca didn't appear that night for my first family dinner—burnt beans on toast—much to Dad's irritation. I wasn't hungry anyway. Afterwards, I begged off watching TV to go unpack and take a long shower to clear my head.

When I finally emerged Blanca was kneeling on my bed, a large book at her feet, admiring the dreamcatcher where I had hung it on the wall over my headboard. I watched her silently from the bedroom door. We were physically very alike: same height, same slender frame, same auburn hair and matching freckles on our noses, cheeks and shoulders. But she had grown over our summer apart. She was becoming a strong, confident young woman. She was leaving me behind.

"I wondered when Mum was going to give you this," she said quietly without turning around, twirling a little feather between thumb and forefinger.

"Why do you always *know* stuff?" I sighed sarcastically. She had a long track record in this department.

"I don't *always* know anything," she grumbled, shaking her head and rolling her eyes at me. "Stop saying that."

I rubbed my hair one last time then tossed the wet towel over the desk chair and sat beside her. "I was an idiot," I admitted, releasing a deep breath. "No more secrets between us, I promise. Forgive me?"

She considered me seriously for a few moments, letting me sweat, then pushed the large book to one side. "Deal," she said and hugged me tightly.

"Soooo," I said at length, breaking our somewhat sentimental embrace before it got to me again. "Dad's got house rules, apparently." I raised my eyebrows in mock shock.

"Look, you need to ease up on him. He's really sorry; he never meant to hurt you," Blanca explained, stroking my arm. I shrugged and looked away.

"Seriously, give him a chance." I didn't respond. "Or not." She threw her arms in the air at my stubbornness and walked over to fold the wet towel. "Antagonise him, wind him up instead if you want to discuss father issues with a shrink in ten years. Bring hundreds of boys back to the house—"

"Any idea where I can find these fabled hordes of Oban gays?" I snapped angrily. She gawked at me, shocked by my outburst. "I mean," I sighed and adjusted my tone. "You'd think it was only a matter of hours before a queue forms at the door." She folded her arms over her chest, unimpressed.

Of course, I couldn't bring boys home. That was a given. But I'd never had a boyfriend in Barcelona, why should here be any different? Besides, I was far too shy.

"Let's drop it," I said after a long, awkward pause. "What's this?" I prodded the huge book beside me.

"I wanted to show you that." My twin perked up and came back to the bed. "D'you remember all those stories Gran used to tell us? About the witch trials and our ancestors?"

"Yeah, I remember her mentioning it once or twice." I rolled my eyes. "Or like every time Mum turned her back."

Gran had gone on and on and on about what she called our 'ancient family heritage' like it was fact. She actually believed there was magic in our blood. We loved her stories when we were wee and, despite Mum's objections, used to run around pretending to cast spells.

"I miss her, too," Bee said softly, lifting my chin. "We can go visit her soon. Mum doesn't have to know."

"So, what's Gran got to do with your book?"

"Well, I've done some researching into our family tree since I got back," she explained excitedly, "and Gran's old stories were true! One of our ancestors was burned for witchcraft in the 1600s."

I was surprised and somewhat impressed. Gran was an eccentric old lady—almost 70 by now—and Mum always made her out to be half-deranged. She was always our favourite.

"It's actually really interesting." Blanca rifled through the book's already battered pages enthusiastically, speaking in a blur. "Here!" She thrust it towards me, pointing to a particular passage. "She was our great-great-great-great grandmother. Well, a lot more greats than that, but you get the picture. And she was a triplet." She blinked at me expectantly, waiting for my jaw to hit the floor. "Sort of like us!" she prompted.

That probably needs some explaining. Technically, Blanca is my slightly-older twin. But our cousin Bobby was born only a few hours before that on the exact same day in the exact same little Oban hospital. With Bobby spending almost every holiday in Barcelona, we were so close as kids we somehow got it into our heads there were three twins instead of two. Mum tried to set us straight, but Gran and Aunt Ella encouraged it shamelessly. In the end, it stuck, and we'd seen ourselves that way ever since.

"I was sure he'd come say hi tonight," I said quietly

and more than a little disappointed.

"He's having a hard time," Bee conceded with a mighty heave of her shoulders. "You know how he bottles things up."

"I know. I still can't believe Aunt Ella's gone," I sighed, remembering getting the news just before Easter. It'd been a rough year for us all. "He must really miss her."

"He does, not that he'd ever admit it. But right now the problem's Samantha," Blanca said. She stood up and helped me fold down the covers on my bed. "She dumped him, totally out of the blue, for another guy."

"No!" I gasped and stopped in my tracks gaping at her. "But they seemed so into one another when they visited last Christmas!"

"I know, right?" my sister agreed. "No one knows why. She won't talk to him. Won't talk to anyone."

"He won't speak to me either," I said very quietly, placing the extra pillows in the corner. "I don't know how to—"

"You two will have to sort it out on our own," she said, pursing her lips. "Leave me out of it. Anyway, the book!"

She immediately launched back into her explanation before I could object, giving me the run down on her weeks of research. The barrage of information would have made my head spin, but my mind was already elsewhere.

"Wait! Stop!" I finally interrupted, holding up my

hands. "You don't believe any of this, do you?"

"No, of course I don't," she sighed, confirming what I already knew: Bee wasn't prone to wild flights of fancy. I was the dreamer; she was practical. Reclining against my headboard, the book open in her lap, her brow furrowed just like Dad, I thought I saw the slightest hint of a scowl. "But it'd be nice, wouldn't it?"

"I'll say," I snorted. "I could sure use some super powers!"

She reached over and gave me another big hug. "They're gone now. It'll all be different here, a fresh start. Yeah?"

I nodded and smiled weakly.

"Anyway," she said gently, giving me a thoughtful look like I might break if she made any sudden move. "I'll let you get to bed. But have a look at the book. Witches or no witches, it's really interesting."

She set it on my bedside table, tucked the duvet around me and planted a sweet kiss on my forehead before disappearing downstairs to her new bedroom.

"*Witchcraft in Scotland in the Middle Ages*," I read the title aloud. Not exactly a catchy title. I opened the hard cover without picking it up and flicked through a few pages. God, I hoped she didn't become obsessed with this family tree and witchcraft business. I knew how much she liked a project. But I'd worry about that tomorrow, I decided, snuggling down under the covers.

The wind and rain welcomed me to the Highlands that night, blitzing the roof and windows until the whole house groaned with unfamiliar sounds. I rolled onto my side away from the window and covered my head with the duvet, but sleep eluded me well into the wee small hours. When at last it came it was filled with nightmares that woke me frightened and panting again and again. Until, well past 3 a.m., when I got back to sleep for the fourth or fifth time, the dreams changed.

*

Ross J. Noble is an aspiring author working on his first novel, The Wisher, *of which 'Homecoming', is the opening chapter. A graduate of Heriot-Watt University, Edinburgh and Université Sorbonne Nouvelle (ESIT), Paris, he lives in Brussels where he works as a conference interpreter and translator.*

Andrea Rees

For Jorge

PEOPLE ALWAYS SAY it's hard to know when to stop. In the last days, I've come to realize that the stopping part is easy. It's actually harder to know when to start.

And where to start. So, for the sake of starting, I'll begin two Saturdays ago, after I navigated the narrow stairs and stepped off the 81 tram at the Guillaume Tell stop in St. Gilles. Saint Gilles is not a commune that I know well. Audrey lives there. She's always lived in that area, as after moving to Brussels, I've always lived either in or next to Woluwe-Saint-Lambert. Daniel picked this commune; I'm not sure why, perhaps there was no real reason, and I've just stuck with it. I suppose like my old cardigan, the beige one with the chipped pearly buttons and the frayed sleeves, it brought me comfort through familiarity.

The doors unfolded closed with their flapping sound behind me, and as the streetcar screeched away, I surveyed my surroundings. The sun was extraordinarily strong that day, but rather than bringing the narrow brick and stone buildings to life, the light only emphasized just how dreary and gray Brussels really is. I walked a few steps down rue Théodore Verhaegen and then turned left on rue du Fort. Street of the strong. A place where I don't belong. There are more Moroccan people living in this neighbourhood than in mine, and I'm ashamed to admit that even though they were just going about their daily business, being surrounded by so many headscarves and the throaty growl of Arabic made me feel uncomfortable. I excused myself with the idea that I was a female, in a fragile state, on her own in unfamiliar terrain, but being honest, I'm sure I would have felt the same way even if I had been feeling better. Please know, I am not proud of this.

I'm not sure if I've mentioned Fernando before. He is a member of a collective of audio-visual artists called SICLOP. They are focused on art, on creation, on trying to see things in a different way, and on that Saturday, they were throwing a party to celebrate the end of their three-month residency and installation at the Fortissimo cultural space.

Fernando is originally from Porto. He is a short man, just a little taller than me, with wavy hair, a full but trim beard, and twinkling eyes. I met him through Audrey who is good friends with one of his ex-girlfriends. I accompanied her to the screening of a short film he had made, with the same ex-girlfriend, which was being shown in Brussels just before moving to the festival in Cannes. After, I saw him, from time to time, at a dinner party or a gathering and we became Facebook friends. I don't actually know him very well. But I do know that he is talented and kind.

The exterior of the four-storey Fortissimo is decorated with large, black, musical notes, each one about the size of a guitar. They were fitted in between the numerous windows, and I struggled to imagine how they would sound if I played them on my piano, but I couldn't focus. I think now they were probably just single, lonely, unconnected tones. I followed the narrow entrance into a small courtyard. It resembled a cell with glass walls. To my left was a packed café; the sounds of chatter and laughter, glasses clinking, forks clattering against plates, and the smell of warming quiche, all seeped into my cramped space through an open window. In front of me, there seemed to be a small, bright, but empty library, and to the right of that, a less illuminated, almost empty exhibition space. Some of the strange faces in the café glanced at me while others peered, like I was a fish in a bowl, feeling sorry for me, trapped in my own small world and knowing I would never be part of theirs. I stared over my shoulder, at the route I had just taken, and then at the three doors in front of me. I took one step back, but then, after a long pause, took many more forward.

The library was even smaller on the inside, and it opened right up onto the exhibition area next door. I'm not sure if it was the raw wooden tables or the way some of the lights cast long shadows over the walls, but something about it reminded me of that bar where we used to hang out. As I continued to look around, I saw Fernando straightening a photo on the far wall across from me. He was just turning around as I reached him.

"Hey! Fernando," I said and mustered a smile. The belt of my black cashmere coat was cinched tightly around my waist, and my blue scarf, which I had bought because it brings out my eyes, was wrapped snugly around my neck, like a person who was about to leave rather than one who had just arrived.

"Hi!" he said, and while he too was smiling, his eyes were looking at me inquisitively.

"It's Alex… It's been ages since I've seen you."

His full lips pushed his beard aside as they opened up into a broad grin and he leaned forward, momentarily taking one of my hands in his and brushing his prickly cheek against my smooth one in a standard Brussels kiss. "Thanks for coming," he chimed. "Yes, it's been a while. At Giulia's I think."

I did think he was cute, but I again remembered what Audrey had told me about him. How he's not very selective and gets obsessive about his girlfriends and always struggles to let go once it's over. She said he looks fun and light, but really he's heavy. "Yeah, I think you're right. The last time I saw you was at the dinner at Giulia's. Thanks for inviting me. Am I bit early?" I asked, looking around and of course glad there was hardly anyone there. The cold, predominantly stark concrete walls extended further back than I'd initially guessed, but even at their deepest point, they surrounded only a few more people.

"It officially started at five," he said in his soft, warm English flecked with a slight Portuguese accent. "I invited all of my Facebook friends, but I think most of them will come later for the dancing. I think Giulia said she might be able to come, but later too. And Audrey's away."

"Yeah, I think so too. At a wedding or something." Actually, I knew for sure that Audrey was at a wedding and that Giulia probably wouldn't come later, and that John had a birthday party, and that every person I knew in Brussels had plans that evening. Jorge, you know I had wanted to go to the party with someone. But you don't know that when I couldn't find anyone, I almost decided not to go. I only went because I promised you.

A woman came up behind Fernando and whispered in his ear. He nodded and said, "Okay" to her before turning back to me. "Have a look around. I did all the films, one of my colleagues did the photos. There are some installations downstairs, and there'll be some performance pieces later. I need to help them get ready. The theme of everything is resistance."

I toured the cavernous main floor first. There wasn't much to see. There seemed to be more dust on the walls than art. And I had a sense that what was there was just not trying hard enough, or perhaps too hard. But I lingered over everything, even over the set of Polaroid's, taken in different cities in the world, that to me, although absent of people, resembled nothing more than vacation photos and I couldn't see any connection to the theme. But as I wandered, I remember thinking that as my first party after Daniel, this was a good one to come to. The art, although it wasn't much, still gave me something to focus on, and provided an obvious topic of conversation, making it easier to chat with the few people I did encounter. Although I must be honest, throughout it all, I loosened neither the belt of my coat nor my scarf.

I wish I could remember the very first party I ever went to and how I felt. Have I always been intimidated by large gatherings of people? I could go to parties with Daniel though. He had seemed to understand and had always been there. When the fear got to be too much, when the strangeness of everyone and everything crowded in too close around me, I would go to him, and he would take my hand in his or let me sit on his knee for a few minutes. It was as if his energy recharged a force field around me.

I read somewhere that when someone loses a life partner, the hardest thing is the sense that they have literally lost half of their mind. That over the years, their brain has adapted and merged with their partner's so much so that each one does and remembers half of the things that need to be done and remembered. The loss of this has never gone away, nor has that sense that half of my body, half of who I am is missing too.

In the basement, the focal point was a film of Fernando's, projected onto the main wall. I watched the whole thing, even though I was bored silly, I remember nothing about its content, and then eventually inched my way up the steep, treacherous stairs with a strong sense that I had seen it all and that it would be acceptable to leave soon. As I reached the top, cooler air tickled my face and a whole mix of sounds—doors banging, voices rising and falling, electronic equipment squealing—pierced my ears and made me shudder. During my absence, the place had filled up, and two microphones had been set up, surrounded by a small staging area.

"What's happening?" I asked a tall skinny blonde guy in a black, draped-open leather jacket who was standing alone. He had a luminous, friendly face, and I was sure, much younger than me.

"There's supposed to be some kind of performance soon," he said in perfect English. "That's all I know."

"Are you here on your own?"

"Yeah, my friends are supposed to come, but I don't know when. And you?"

Of course, I was relieved he was solo. At least for a little while, I had found a 'plus one'. "Yeah, I'm a friend of Fernando's. I came to be supportive. I have a dinner later though, so I can't stay too late." I was lying and laying the foundation for my out that I could engage when I needed it. "Do you know Fernando?"

"Not really. I've met him a few times, but we have a lot of common friends."

"I'm Alex by the way," I said extending my hand.

"Christian," he replied as we shook. "Nice to meet you."

"Nice to meet you too. Where are you from? Your English is perfect. I can't detect any accent."

"Oh, thanks! I'm German."

"Oh, I love Germany. Been to Aachen and Dusseldorf...oh and to Cologne, and of course Berlin. Many times. I love Berlin. Where in Germany are you from?"

"You wouldn't know it. It's a small town between Munich and Cologne. And you? Where are you from?"

"Michigan. But I've been living in Brussels for almost ten years now. I have dual nationality. So I'm Belgian too now. Do you live in Brussels?"

"Yes, for eight years. I came for work. I work in a hotel."

"No kidding. Many years ago I tried to get a job in a hotel. Didn't have any luck though. I loved the idea of all these strangers, with their own, separate lives and stories, coming together under one roof."

A huge grin popped onto his face. "Yes, yes," he said enthusiastically.

Although I can't feel the exact feeling now, I do remember at that moment, for a brief moment, I was oblivious to the constantly growing crowd around us and had a sense of connection. And Jorge, you know how much I love that feeling of connection, that feeling that was always so powerful, uniquely powerful, whenever we talked. I think now it probably isn't dissimilar to that feeling I used to get whenever I looked at a Rothko painting. Kind of like a brain massage I think. I wish I could feel it again now. But I can't. It's impossible.

"What hotel do you work for?" I asked. But before he could answer, the sound of two fingers tapping a microphone thumped throughout the room and brought every pocket of chatter to an immediate, sharp end. All heads turned towards the makeshift stage and the woman who had caused the noise. She was about my height and slender but had your complexion. She was dark with olive skin, deep brown eyes, and a short, shiny black bob. Her face was weathered but not from age. She was wearing skinny black jeans and a flowing grey shirt. The smell of mint invaded my nose, and I glanced to see Fernando standing next to me with a mug in his hands.

"Je suis une artiste Iranienne," she said into the microphone, her voice and face revealing no emotion. Her words seemed at first to hover over us, and then suddenly, crash on our heads.

She said the same thing again, in the same way, and then walking very slowly up the rough, uneven staircase I had manoeuvred not so long before, another woman appeared. She was stark naked. She was also dark and bore a striking resemblance to the other. But this time, I could see that her full, wiry pubic hair was as thick and black as the hair on her head, and her full breasts hung low on her chest, and rhythmically swayed along with her hips as she walked. Although she made no sound, she was music.

All eyes were on her, and Jorge, I wondered what you would have thought. And what the men were thinking. Were they titillated? Was it even possible for them to see her as an asexual piece of art? I stole a peek at Christian's face to my one side, and then to Fernando's on my other, but they told me nothing.

When she reached the other microphone, the one to the right of her colleague, she said, *"Elle est une artiste Iranienne."*

And then the other woman said, "Je suis une artiste Iranienne."

They went back and forth like this for what seemed to be ten minutes, but perhaps it wasn't that long at all. Perhaps the nudity had created a discomfort in me that had made it seem longer. I still wonder, how did she feel being so exposed? Strong? Or vulnerable? And then she slowly made her way back down the staircase from which she had come, with her colleague not far behind.

Once they had disappeared, I said to Fernando, "I'm not sure I get that. Was the nudity meant to shock?" I had wanted to use the word 'arouse' but stopped myself at the last minute.

"I don't know," he said. "I can't explain. I don't know their idea behind it. But there's a new installation downstairs now. Come, I'll show you."

I looked at Christian.

"I should wait here for my friends," he said.

"Would you like some tea?" Fernando asked.

We both declined.

The new installation was in a pitch-black room, sealed off by a curtain, in which sounds of ships and the sea were playing. Fernando and I squeezed our way in, and each found a place against the wall. He still had his mug, and the smell of mint now mingled with sweat. We listened to the cry of seagulls, the roar of the ocean, the lapping of waves, and the bellow of a ship's horn, but no matter how hard I tried, no matter how much I wanted it, I just couldn't imagine myself there. It wasn't the sights I was missing, but the smell. That scent that's unlike any other, of the salty ocean air. It's a scent that when I'd been away from the ocean for too long, I used to crave. Daniel was like that too; there were all those times when we were married that I stood on a beach, with the wind whipping my hair, holding his clothes, even on the coldest of days. Smelling the air and being close to the water had never been enough for him, he had had to also totally immerse himself.

Suddenly, I didn't want to be in that dark room anymore, and I tapped Fernando on the arm so that he would know that I was leaving. I was surprised when I stepped past the curtain and realized he had followed me.

"That was nice," I said being polite. "But I don't get how that connects to the theme. To resistance."

"It doesn't," Fernando replied.

When we arrived back upstairs, Christian was still alone, and he said something to Fernando that I couldn't make out—the music and chatter in the room had gotten incredibly loud. As I watched the two men talk to each other, both very attractive, but physical opposites—as Christian was tall, Fernando was short; as Christian was fair, Fernando was dark; as Christian was polished, Fernando was spontaneous, textured—it seemed that they grew in size. Suddenly, even Fernando seemed to be an unreachable giant to me. And as I looked around the room, all of the men appeared that way. "It doesn't matter that I find them attractive," I thought. "That I want to know them, to love them. Once they really get to know me, they'll reject me and leave me. Just like Daniel did. My love is not enough. I am not enough. I will never be enough."

My eyes fell to my watch. I stared at the second hand with its jerky movements, trying to plod its way forward, and when eventually I looked up again, I saw that Christian and Fernando had stopped talking and were gazing past me. A blast of icy air struck us as the main door was held open. I shivered. A new group was arriving, and a pretty brunette in a purple beret and grey pea coat waved at Christian. I turned back to face the two guys. "I'm sorry, it's time for me to go. Meeting some friends for dinner," I said.

"Thanks so much for coming," Fernando said and took my hand and kissed my cheek as he'd done when I'd arrived. Again, I felt his beard scratch my skin.

"Nice to meet you," Christian and I said in unison as we shook hands.

My coat and scarf were still tightly sealed, and I made my way through the crowd and stepped out into the dark, cold night. Alone. I will always be alone. I managed to hold back my tears until I got home, and then I cried for days.

Jorge, my first intention had been to write you a letter, but it didn't feel right. We've always shared stories, so why shouldn't this be one too? It's taken almost all of my strength, but it feels better like this.

I know I've told you this before, but I want to tell you again, meeting you has been one of the luckiest things that has happened to me. I'm sure I wouldn't have survived this long otherwise. It wasn't just having someone to really talk to, to really connect with. Being there for you also helped me. Before you left for Buenos Aires, I thought I was going to make it. And I wanted you to see that I kept my word, that I did try. But the sadness is back; it lays on me now like a thousand bricks in a never-ending night. You know how sometimes you just know things? I just know it will always be like this for me now. I am broken.

Forever broken. People always say it's hard to know when to stop. In the last days, I've come to realize that the stopping part is easy. And it's time for me to stop now. I know you know what I mean. Please don't feel bad. You had to leave. I hope your dad is doing much better. I'm telling you this because in our short friendship, I have always told you everything, and I've never told anyone else everything. Alex.

*

Andrea Rees: *Originally from Canada, Andrea has lived in Brussels for more than a decade. She is currently working on a novel which blends memoir and fiction, and is collaborating on a variety of other creative projects.*

Nicholas Parrott

The Seule Valley; Tibet of the Basque Country

An extract from the forthcoming book: En passant: A voyage along the Pyrenees

La Cave de Verna

The gorges of the Seule Valley have been on tourist itineraries for more than a century and were already listed in many of the nineteenth-century tourist guides to the Pyrenees. Hilaire Belloc, author of one of the best known and most comprehensive of them, was here and explored all of them. At that time Mauleon and Tardets-Sorholus were connected by a tram line, Mauleon had a railway station, the roads beyond Tardets were primitive tracks, and there was no identifiable path beyond Saint Engrâce. Belloc tried to cross from the Seule into the next valley but failed to find his way. The valley was a *cul-de-sac*, not for nothing known as the 'Tibet of the Basque Country' as it was so remote. Today it is still remote, and there are no longer train or tram lines in the valley, although there are now two roads beyond Saint Engrâce, both of which help feed the ski trade in the winter months. What Hilaire Belloc, and nobody else at the time, did not know was the scale of the cave systems that lie inside these mountains.

It wasn't until after the Second World War that the first details of this huge hydrological system began to emerge. Underneath the mountains there is a complex of underground waterways and caverns that absorbs the water from the tops of the mountains, filtering it for miles before releasing it in the canyons and gorges of the Seule Valley. Thirteen underground rivers have so far been discovered, the longest with a drop of almost fifteen hundred metres before disgorging itself into the valley below Saint Engrâce. So far, more than 400 kilometres of caves, shafts and chambers have been explored.

Norbert Casteret, who is most famous for using green dye to locate the source of the Garonne on the Spanish side of the border, is credited with being the leader of the team that first discovered this complex. In 1950, an expedition he was leading had spent a few days just below the Col du Pierre St Martin without discovering any cave systems. On the last day of the expedition, a team member dejectedly threw a stone into an opening. It audibly clattered into an abyss and started a flurry of speleological activity that continues to this day. They were out of supplies so had to wait until the following year to return, when they made the first descent into Chasm Lépineux, to a depth of 320 metres, the deepest-ever cave exploration recorded at the time. The following year tragedy struck. The winch and cable system used to descend into the cave snapped, sending Marcel Loubens hurtling fifteen metres downwards to a ledge. He broke his jaw-bone and his spinal cord and fell into a coma. The other climbers got word out and the attempts to get him out of the cave alive, supported by Air Force helicopters and a troop of boy scouts from Lyon who ferried supplies to the inaccessible site, lasted three days, attracting the world's press to this mountaintop, and involved the first-ever subterranean blood transfusion. Unfortunately, it was unsuccessful, and he was interred in the *gouffre* for two years until his body was exhumed.

Undaunted, the team returned the following year, a few months after Everest was first conquered. A team of four cavers reached the bottom of the chimney, 734 metres deep, twice as deep than any caving team had ever been before. They spent twenty-four hours crawling over rocks, through tunnels and along stream beds to eventually find themselves in a cavern so huge that their torches could not pick out its walls or roof. They imagined that they had ventured back out above the surface and it was night-time. It was only when one of them checked his watch that they realised that it was daytime and that they were still underground and had discovered a chamber larger than any known to man. They named it *La Cave de Verna* after the troop of Boy Scouts from Lyon that had helped them the previous year. After sixty or so more years of underground exploration, La Cave de Verna has now dropped down the rankings. It's now the 17th largest cave in the world, but it retains one distinction: it is the largest cave in the world that is open to the public.

Our tour guide is Eric, tall, lean, athletic. It's near the end of the afternoon, and the minibus driver has knocked off work for the day, so we form a makeshift convoy of five vehicles outside the tourist office's reception area. It's a bank weekend holiday in Spain, just a few miles away as the crow flies, so I am the only non-Hispanic speaking person in the group. I'm driving the lead vehicle with Eric in the passenger seat, giving me instructions and keeping one eye on the line of vehicles behind us to make sure we don't lose anyone. On reflection, I would rather he had driven. We leave the car park, drop through past the village church and then further down to the very bottom of the valley before climbing up the shady side of the mountain and onto a single-lane cement track. At this point, things get positively Himalayan. I've been almost all the way across the Pyrenees, visited the Alps and Dolomites and lived in Wales, but I have never before seen such a steep or narrow road in Europe.

'You need to go into second after this bend', says Eric. 'This is where all the women go 'eek'. I almost did too. This was followed by a precipitous descent and another ascent up to a small clearing with enough parking space for our convoy. Eric unlocks a cabin that is used to store windproof jackets and safety helmets. He gives a safety briefing and advises us to take the jackets and helmets, as it is very cold inside the mountain and the ceiling is low in some places. At this point, he gives me, the tallest member of the group, a pointed look. We walk across the parking lot to a metal doorway in the side of the mountain. It is unassuming. It could be the entry to a cheese store. There are no signs indicating that you are about to enter the world's largest show cave. This enterprise is very low key.

Today visitors to La Cave de Verna no longer have to follow the route of the original explorers, down a 700-metre chimney by winch and rope and then scrambling along a subterranean river bed. In the 1950s EDF, the French State electricity company, blasted a tunnel through the mountain hoping to construct a hydro-electric project inside it. Three years of drilling and tunnelling and millions of Francs later they realised that the water flow wasn't sufficient for the project to be viable. The technicians locked the tunnel down, only allowing limited access to licensed cavers. The project was condemned as environmental vandalism and a massive waste of public funds, but thirty years later, with improved technology, a private company decided to have another go. They found a viable solution, building a head reservoir and installing almost two kilometres of pressurised piping that now feeds a small HEP station below Saint Engrâce. The scheme is owned by the commune and has generated enough revenue to put in the infrastructure needed to open the cave to the public and create a second revenue stream.

The tunnel is a concrete-paved corridor that has been blasted out of the rock. There are iron railings along its sides, and a fierce wind howls through it. It is unearthly, like being in a dystopian science fiction movie, I feel like I am no longer on the planet I woke up on this morning.

We eventually reach the cavern. It is simply one of the wonders of the Pyrenees, if not the world. The main chamber is almost two hundred metres high, and it has a diameter of two hundred and fifty metres. One could build nine Notre Dame Cathedrals in here and still have space left over. It is awe-inspiring. Eric invites us to shout and whoop to create an echo call, which the Spanish holidaymakers' kids are particularly enthusiastic about. It resonates around the chamber for tens of seconds until Eric lowers his hands signalling us to stop. After, in the silence, the dark and the cold are overwhelming. Eric goes over to a lighting panel and activates a relayed switching system which progressively illuminates from where we are standing, all the cave all the way to the back and the top. Life-size mannequins in hi-visibility waterproofs have been strategically placed at various distances into the cave. Without these mannequins, it would be impossible to absorb how vast this cave is. The most distant mannequin is a fraction of the size of my little fingernail.

In the 1990s a group of students got permission to launch a full-size hot air balloon inside the cavern. This venture required considerable tenacity, with logistical back-up from the French army, who used donkeys and horses to drag hundreds of kilos of tack up the mountainside (at the time there was no paved track to the cave) and along the cave's corridor. Feeding and accommodating the whole crew was a venture that involved co-operation from the entire village of Saint Engrâce and beyond. The photos and video of this expedition show the balloon nearing the cavern's ceiling, looking no bigger than a small, bright, red moth on the ceiling of a hotel room.

One might think that nothing could live in such an inhospitable environment, but the cave is home to two species of minute invertebrates, blind, and with no pigmentation: *Aphoenops loubensi* and *Aphoenops cabidochei.* They need an atmosphere saturated with humidity in order to survive: the females lay a solitary egg from which a small larva hatches which, unlike insects that live on the surface, immediately metamorphoses into an adult, without feeding. One of these species lives on plant matter, the other is carnivorous, but I forget which is which. Either way, there is a rather delicate population dynamic to maintain. The cave's guardians nourish and nurse a small colony of these insects in the shelter of a pile of stones in the area accessible to the public. Eric lifts up a few stones before finding some moving around. They are tiny, not much to look at really, but knowing what I am looking at is moving: possibly the rarest creatures I have seen, or will ever, see. Eric takes care when putting the stone back not to crush any and commit an act of ecological genocide.

Eric is giving the commentary in Spanish as I am the only non-Hispanic in the group. I am surprised how much better I understand scientific Spanish than conversational Spanish. I'm managing to fill in the gaps quite well. While walking between the various viewing points, Eric gives me a summary in English.

On the way back out Eric ushers us all into a small antechamber built into the side of the tunnel. He turns out the tunnel lights and returns to us finding his way with a torch and then extinguishes it.

'This is how dark it is underground. Put your hands in front of your eyes and see if you can see them'.

None of us can.

Eric tells us about people who have been stuck in caves when their lights failed and had to wait for two days before being rescued by colleagues. A collective shiver goes down our spines. To be stuck in the cold and dark like that must be truly frightening and uncomfortable, not even knowing if anyone is going to be able to find you, not even able to walk a few steps to take a pee without knowing where your footing is.

Eric rekindles the light and, while it is still very dark in the tunnel, we breathe a collective sigh of relief at being able to see again. The wind in the tunnel is on our backs now, less chilling than before and driving us towards the exit as if the underground gods are trying to hasten our departure from their sacred realm. On the way out I fail to see a low patch of the rock ceiling and bump my head hard against it. If not for the safety helmet I could easily have concussed myself. As it is, it makes me dizzy for a few minutes, and I drop behind the others. Eric, sensing something is amiss, comes back to check I'm okay, telling the others to wait for us.

It's a huge relief to get out of the cave, to step out into the blindingly bright sunshine, feel a warm wind on my face and hear the birds sing and leaves rustle. This is how fairy tales end, this is how the hobbits must have felt when finally emerging from Moria into Lothlorien. Am I being a drama queen? Maybe! But I had a genuine sense of fear and foreboding in the caves, one I've never felt before: even the first time I flew. And our visit had only lasted a little more than an hour.

Eric asks me if I am alright to drive back down the mountain and I nod assent. On the way Eric has fewer concerns about losing convoy members, so we get a chance to talk a bit more. We both try to place each other's accents. His, it turns out, is Afrikaans, and he thinks I sound Dutch. He is an adrenaline junkie. On his days off he goes exploring the depths of those caves, hoping that one day a piece of subterranean landscape will be named after him. When he's not inside the mountain, he's on top of it, snowboarding, or chasing tidal bores on his surfboard. He tells me about when as a youth he once sailed around the Caribbean and later wrote a book about it. His trip ended when he ran out of money and had to sell the boat.

'I wrote about all those my adventures and my friends said it was really good.'

'Friends do, but why don't you try to publish it?'

'I thought running out of money was a bad way to finish a travel book.'

'That's how many travel adventures finish, look at 'On the Road', Jack Kerouac only came back from Mexico because he was sick and out of funds'.

I saw something like a gleam in Eric's eye at that point. But I suspect he'd rather be climbing a V5 crag next weekend than sitting in front of a dusty manuscript or a laptop.

Tardets—Sorholus

The next day, as on every day during my stay here on the campsite on the edge of Tardets, the sun rises bright and strong from behind the hill, shining into my chalet at 9.00, almost on the dot. After being deep underground in a cave yesterday I dreamt about cold and dark places during the night —so the sunshine is more welcome than usual. But, this being a Monday, my wake-up call is earlier and ruder than over the weekend: a chainsaw kicks into action on the camp at eight thirty on the dot. The whining noise is soon joined by two others, calling each other across the valley like a trio of amorous metallic owls. I'd already become aware that this valley isn't a peaceful rural idyll. Even on weekends, there is a four-times-daily procession of farm machinery going from farm to field and back bringing in the maize, the last cut of hay, next winter's wood or moving livestock. The variety in this farm machinery is astounding. There's a brand new mega-harvester: when I see that kind of machine and think about how much it must cost it seems to give the lie to farmers' claims of being in permanent financial crisis. There is another harvester that looks more a medieval siege machine with huge spikes retracted above the body of the vehicle and what looks like a battering ram at the front: probably for forestry work. And there goes the old farmer with a bedraggled straw hat, pootling by on what looks like a no-more than four horsepower tractor with a piece of corrugated iron mounted on four poles to protect him from the rain and sun. That must have been among the first generation of agricultural machinery to be brought into this valley. And that wasn't so long ago. In Pierre Benoit's 1954 collection of photos of the Basque Country, most of the agricultural work was still being done with draft power and farmers would more often have a horse and cart than a car or tractor. 'Just popping down to the shops, dear' would have been far harder when you had to harness the horse to the carriage first but, then, people were a lot more self-reliant in those days.

Tardets is a charming little village. Hilaire Belloc was taken by it more than a hundred years ago, writing of its architectural charm and the friendliness of the people. That has not changed at all in that time. The inhabitants and traders of Tardets are some of the friendliest I have met on this trip along the Pyrenees. But the hotel where Hilaire stayed is now derelict, and the whole village is visibly shrinking, like an ageing man. The houses and hotels on the perimeters of the village are dilapidated, uncared for, or boarded up. The evidence is not just anecdotal: in 1962 the population of the commune, consisting of a dozen or so hamlets clustered around the main village, exceeded 1100 people. At the last census, in 2013, it was down to less to 600. This commune has one of the highest rates of population loss anywhere in France. My conversations with people almost inevitably turn to their brothers, sisters, sons or daughters who have moved away: to the coast, to larger cities or even abroad. There's a longing in their tone. They want them to do well in their new lives—but their absence is still deeply felt, especially perhaps those who are furthest away, for whom the journey home for feast-days and family reunions are both costly and time-consuming.

But it's also a village that keeps its traditions. Here,

every February, they celebrate *Les Mascarades Souletines,* a local variant of Mardi Gras that takes place over several weekends. It takes place in and around the thirty-six villages and hamlets scattered along the valley, although the finale is always in Tardets. The photos of the event look positively pagan, bacchanalian. Some of the men are wearing what can best be described as pyjamas made out of material that came out of the curtain section at Biba. Their costumes are topped off with berets with a fringe of pink or yellow pom-poms. Others have daubed their faces with charcoal and are wearing stag horns and outsize cow bells strapped to their backs that jingle with every step as they process around the square. Others are in drag. The women's dress is more conventional; their attire more uniform: white shoes, blue gaiters, white stockings, scarlet, knee-length dresses, with white trim and pinafore and elaborately embroidered blue jackets and hats. They look like a Dixie Band, except that instead of carrying brass instruments they dance in the village square, each one taking her turn to see who can produce the most complex and sophisticated soft-shoe shuffle and win the most applause from the audience.

That is still four months away, but I'm already in anticipation of it. It feels like a really authentic piece of local folklore, one that people do for themselves rather than to bring in the tourist Euros.

Sure, visitors come to watch and join the festivities

but, in the videos I find on the internet, they seem to be outnumbered by local participants. Reading articles and watching the videos about this event leads me to reflect on a very real paradox about Basque culture: the Basques are fervently Catholic, yet also deeply animistic, shamanistic and pagan. They carry a strong tradition of sorcery and beliefs in, and reverence for, the spirits of the earth, water, animals and the nature around them. This paradox is most evident in the Basque cross: a hybrid of Christian and pagan traditions. Each branch of the cross is like an apostrophe with the tips joined at the centre. Besides the Christian symbolism, it also represents the passing of the seasons and the four winds. You see it everywhere in Basque architecture, carved into doors and gateposts, in the shape of windows on stairwells and on placemats and mugs. It's uniquely Basque and quite ubiquitous.

Les Mascarades Souletines are basically a courtship ritual for local young people, timed to occur before the hard work of preparing fields for the spring sowing or taking livestock up to higher pastures. And though these activities are less central to people's livelihoods today than preparing beds or camping sites for the influx of summer tourists, the festival still persists. It's a way for the young people, spread across these scattered villages and hamlets, working on farms most of the summer, to familiarise. And, as they throw this party in different villages over the spread of several weeks, it's a not a one-night fling but a chance to build new relationships, friendships and networks. A week before, in the next valley to the east, I had visited the museum in Arête and seen photos of a similar bacchanal that was discontinued in the 1990s because of a declining population and lack of interest. Here in Tardets they have managed to keep it alive and keep it real.

Annoyed by the noise of chainsaws on the campsite, I head into the village for lunch. There's a great little café on the corner of the square that does good value lunchtime formulas. It's an elegant, old-style, cafe with wooden panelling and large mirrors behind the bar. It probably hasn't had a makeover since it was built and is much the better for that. The staff seem to know me already after just three visits and are chatty. A few days before I had encountered a group of four British bikers buying themselves cheese and bread in the local deli, complaining that there was nowhere open that evening to eat. I took them down to this café, and they had apparently ordered the 'full Monty' so today I unexpectedly get a *pichét* of wine as 'commission'. Today's set-menu is local veal, cooked in a milky, peppery, sauce. It's delicious and reminds me of the 'traffic-jam' I had encountered last week, high on the mountain road that descends from the pass below Ohri, when a farmer was moving his herd of thirty or so cows and calves from one meadow to the next.

I need a new pocket knife, so after lunch I head to the *quincaillerie*. The door is open, but there's no-one there. I go in, have a look around and then go to the back of the shop hoping to attract someone's attention. There's a curtained-off section half-hiding a kind of therapy room with a massage table, illustrations of chakras and a board describing the types of energetic healing on offer. I go back into the shop and call out to attract someone's attention. No reply. When I come back 15 minutes later the owner a short, well-tanned, blue-eyed man, a few years younger than me, sporting the inevitable Basque beret, has returned.

'I was here fifteen minutes ago, but there was nobody here. Do you often leave your shop open and unattended?'

'Oh, I had to pop out to run an errand. There's no need to worry about locking the shop here. Can I get you something?'

I think of the scale of looting that would occur if one were to do that in the poorer quarters of Brussels that have been my home for the past five years, or any other city for that matter. It's one of the differences between urban and rural living: you don't continually have to worry about locking things. I am distracted from that line of thought as I watch his fingers in constant motion winding a string of black rubber into a little ball.

'What's that?' I ask.

'It will be a pelota ball. They're all hand-made and fetch a lot of money. Do you know pelota? It's our national sport.'

'I saw a game on TV last week. It looks quite fast. Who's the therapist here?'

'Oh, that's me too. I do a few sessions a week.'

I'm impressed. This guy is clearly a polymath—a shopkeeper, therapist and artisan all at the same time. And he has managed to arrange his life so that he can do all three trades from the same spot. I wonder how many other income streams he has.

Multiple job holding is a necessary survival strategy in marginal rural areas—and you can't get much more marginal than Tardets. But multiple jobs can also make the effort of earning a living less of a drudgery. I eventually remember about the knife that I came in to buy and ask to see them. Knives are something you have to hold in order to develop an affinity with. He opens the glass cabinet and invites me to pick one out. I pick out one about nine inches long that, thanks to my 'wood lesson' in the museum in Arête last week, I think is cherry. I ask him, and he confirms it, and I win a few local brownie points. It has four bronze studs set on one side of the handle and a small bronze Basque cross on the other. That's a good omen. The steel looks and feels good quality, but then it should be. The Basque country, one of the world's first industrialized regions, has been making steel for more than two hundred years. This knife is unlikely to rust after a few months, like those dreadful *Opinels*, and he only wants 18 Euros for it. It feels like a bargain.

Across the market square, stands the newly finished tourist office. It's all glass and pine panels: very Scandinavian. One can still smell the varnish. On the top floor there is a museum of Basque folklore. I expect it to be full of drab and dusty artefacts rescued from barn sales or donated by local worthies but get one of the best surprises of this trip. The top floor is white, bright and airy and, rather than being stuffed with ancient folkloric artefacts, it contains an array of cutting-edge po-mo, multi-media installations celebrating and reinterpreting Basque culture and mythology from a 21st-century perspective. I feel like I have stepped out of a Basque valley, with its ancient traditions into a chic urban gallery with a Celtic twist, celebrating reverence for the springs and waterways that sustain people, the *laminak,* androgynous water sprites, half-human half-animal, who are believed to live there—the smugglers, of both goods and people, who knew all the back ways and the hideaway caves and often colluded with local customs officials, and—the 'witches' who were revered and persecuted in equal measure. It is a sensory, impressionistic, experience of Basque culture, rather than a historical narrative of dates and lines of succession, and it leaves an abiding impression.

The best came last. The entrance to the building has a three-storey high vestibule. Hay and straw would have been hoisted up here from the entrance below and used to keep the living quarters insulated during winter and allow the family to 'gravity-feed' the cattle by dropping a bale down whenever needed. The third floor—where I am—is about ten metres above ground level. There is a triple nylon mesh net strung across the atrium. I kick my shoes off, safely stow my new knife safely in a zipped pocket and step out onto the mesh, feeling like I am walking out onto thin air. It's a marvellous feeling: one of being simultaneously suspended and supported. This is a chill-out zone *par excellence*. There's UV lighting above the netting, birdsong drifting into the space from one of the installations inside the gallery, an audiotape of a Pyrenean thunderstorm rattling around the enclosure and a south-facing window looking out over a blue sky with wispy clouds. A fly starts to climb up the window pane, as it climbs higher its wings become increasingly translucent until every vein and vessel is highlighted, picked out by the southerly sun. It gets to the top of the large pane, then flies back down again, trapped behind the glass. Every time it gets close to the top it starts to look like a miniature, living, mandala. It's a transcendental moment. I lose track of how much time I spend lying on that netting, watching the fly repeating the same pattern of movements, trapped on a treadmill of its own creation, while listening to the artificial thunderstorm and birdsong, and seeing the parallel with my own life. They should rent this space out by the hour: it has the restorative powers of an ashram, a spa, a bordello. I think I'm falling in love with this village. Yes, it's in decline, but it's a genteel decline.

On my way back from the village to the campsite, I make a little detour by the river bank. There's a row of buildings, built high on a bluff as a defence against the spring floods and a couple of them have the most ornate balconies imaginable. They look best at this time of day when the late afternoon sunshine illuminates them to full effect. One, in particular, stands out. Buttressed into the wall, it spans the upper two stories of the house and extends over what looks like six rooms, two with open balconies, four being internal extensions. The woodwork is intricate: a mix of whorls and loops—it reminds me of the romantic-period Victorian eaves one sometimes sees in spa towns. But the most stunning thing is its colour: a combination of russet and ochre, it absolutely glows when the late afternoon sunshine picks out every fine point of architectural detail.

Again I am reminded of the Himalayas. I've only seen building styles like this in Himachel Pradesh and Bhutan. That's twice in one week I have made this association. The next day I find I am not alone in making such a seemingly whimsical association. Marie, the owner of the campsite, lent me several books about the Seule and one of them: Pierre-Louis Giannerini's book on love and eroticism in Roman sculpture, has a section about the erotic sculptures that can be found in the church at Saint Engrâce, which he likens to those at Khajuraho in India. *'In the (11th century) church at Saint Engrâce in Haute Soule we can find entangled lovers although the [man's] penis has been cut away by a zealous censor. From close proximity, an elephant regards the scene. What's this? Eastern religion in Cartubrie? Buddhism in the Pyrenees? Try to get your head around that one'.* I flick through the book, and despite my limited French vocabulary, I get the impression that it is one of those join-the-imaginary-dots-and-find-the-hidden-secrets-of-the-Illuminati/Zionist Fathers/Knights of the Templar (make your own choice here).That notwithstanding it doesn't explain how elephants and erotic art managed to find their way into an 11th-century church in the deepest reaches of the Basque Country. I don't think Hannibal even got this far. Tomorrow I will visit the church to try to find out more for myself.

*

Nick Parrott *is a freelance editor and now lives in Hendaye, in the French Basque Country. He is the author of a walking guide to West Yorkshire and co-author of The Real Green Revolution. The piece in this anthology is an excerpt from a work in progress about a journey he made along the Pyrenees, from the Med to the Atlantic. His writings about Hendaye can be found at: the-hendaye-diaries.blogspot.fr*

Ciprian Begu

To the City of Hopes and Steel

We've left behind our bags of sorrow,
gliding forward to the City of Hopes,
to the City of Steel.
My uncle and I smile in awe,
elbows resting on the railing,
mesmerised by endless waters.
He looks at me and in his eyes I see
a twinkling of my father's smile.
I take his hand in mine
and only feel like half an orphan.
Hours on end I spent drawing
the curves of the grand Green Lady, posing
with flames of freedom burning
and frozen still in thickets of metal.
Everywhere around, the sky
opened its halls for business, while
the ocean liner is rocking us ever more Westwards,
towards the City of Hopes,
towards the City of Steel.
Lullabied by the shifting Ocean,

we lose ourselves in dreams of grandeur.
But something's happening...
We look around—the South
has flanked us with a stealth army of clouds
sneaking up on us like bandits.
And now our friend, the Ocean, swells,
and he swells proud, while a wall of water
lifts up our ship, and serves it raw
to the Hurricane.
Eastwards, back Eastwards we are flown,
on the mane of the Winds,
and the hours swirl in a hazy terror.
Eastwards, more Eastwards we do fly,
and the Ocean boils, waters cruel-green,
as dark and gloomy days go by.

*

At last we land on solid ground, we're saved!
But, look! Around us soar,
instead of Lady Liberty—Cathedrals,
and Jesuits praying,
and flocks of merchants selling maize,
and dusty shrubs, and reed-made rugs
hung out to dry, and wells, and chimneys,
and the brown-gray tiles, and now
the Central Market, oh my Lord!
We're back in bloody Gdansk!

The Competitive Edge

Tommy—his first—had been best:
eight feet in one minute and forty-five seconds.
At one and a half, it's outstanding.
His second baby, Jessica, had two left feet.
She fell off after only
ten seconds of ridiculous monkey walk.
Now, he had faith in little Jerry, Jr.:
good ankles, slender for his age, steady eyes,
oblivious to heights.
A year and a half on the day.
He picked him up from the crib
and carried him to the balcony
(he had his mother's eyes),
and stood him up
on the foot-wide railing.
"Hmm. Good balance, all right!
This high up wind speed should be
about thirty miles per hour
out of Northwest."
He peeked over,
eighty storeys down—no bystanders,
"That's good."
And he let his son
stand on his own.
Eager, the man darted

to the other end of the railing:
"Come on, little Jerry, do it for Daddy!
Only ten feet, my boy.
Let's go for the record!"

*Originally published in the poetry collection The
Competitive Edge*

The Consumer

That day
my car was broken so
I bought a train ticket
to go to work.
There, I bought a cup of coffee
to bitter my tongue in
a most pleasurable way.
After, I went into my cubicle
and bought shares in a company,
on the Internet.
That would sure bring me profit
(or so I've been told).
At lunch I had lunch
and bought it myself,
for myself.
After work I bought flowers
for my wife, and toys
for my children,
oh, and on the way, I
also bought another cup
of coffee, for myself.
At home my wife and
my credit card have decided
on a new mortgage deal
for ourselves.

*

That day
my car had long since
been fixed and I drove to work,
but first I bought some gas
at the station, and while there
I also got myself some coffee
for the road.
At work I got paid and went
into my cubicle where
I sold some shares
on the Internet.
These indeed brought me profit
(but not like I'd been told).
At lunch I had lunch and
bought it myself,
for myself.
After work I passed
by the jeweller's and bought
a necklace for my wife and bracelets
for my kids.
At home we ordered pizza
for ourselves and cream puffs
for the kids.

*

My children have bought
a wheelchair for me
and coffee for themselves.
After work they come and

visit me, they buy me
flowers and cream puffs.
They've also paid for
their mother's coffin
and most of the funeral expenses.
Paid by my insurance,
my doctor's opinion
is that I should
rest my eyes and try
to keep them closed
for as long as possible
to prepare for "a possible
impairment."
Other than that
there is no other way.
I've no more hair
and no more cells
to pay with.
I remember all the times
I went to work
and paid a lot
of money for gas
and for coffee.
I also invested
in shares and other instruments,
and even got profit,
but, at the same time, I had
a big mortgage to cover.
I managed to pay it off,

right before my wife died.
Oh, I forget,
I'd been paying for
her flowers right up
until the funeral bouquet.
For a while now
I've stopped buying things
and I'm sitting in the chair my
children bought for me,
keeping my eyes closed
for as long as possible.

*

C.S. Begu has been writing poetry and fiction for 15 years. He's published a few short stories, a poetry collection and is now working on a science fiction and fantasy novel. He lives in Belgium with his wife and son.

Lida Papasokrati

St. Roman the Melodist

This story first appeared in the Geneva Writers' Group anthology Offshoots 14: Writing from Geneva

LISTEN: THERE IS THE SOUND of violins being tuned.

The Church of St. Roman the Melodist is empty on a sunny, weekday afternoon, the air heavy with incense from the candles people have lit in front of the saint's icon. It is a very old icon, painted on blackened wood, of the sixth-century Byzantine saint wearing a red cloak and holding a scroll, his head surrounded by a yellow halo. And look! Suddenly the painting of St. Roman opens his eyes and yawns. He leaps out of his portrait and flies over the pews and out through the door into the churchyard. He gives the church bell a friendly pat that rings over the neighbourhood—and now he's off in the cloudless sky, following the sounds that woke him up: the rustling of sheet music, the clash of a hi-hat, a flute trying out a trill, chairs shuffling, a string snapping followed by a muttered curse. St. Roman flies over the streets of Athens, sprawling inland from the coast like a concrete and asphalt starfish, until he lands on the rooftop of the Thirty-Second Public High School. He leaps from window to window until he locates the source of the noise and smiles excitedly. St. Roman may be the patron saint of church singers, but there's nothing he loves more than a school orchestra.

Rehearsals take place at the school gym, where the students are now busy assembling their instruments, a task more difficult for some than for others. Alex, the double bassist, is struggling to carry his contrabass to his spot at the back of the string section while Stella, the third flute, is hunched over her sheet music, biting her nails. St. Roman sits on top of a music stand as Mrs P., the music teacher, lifts her baton.

In her head, Mrs P. has a class of imaginary students who are polite, dedicated, disciplined, and probably Scandinavian, and these students fall silent the minute she raises her hands. Her real-life students, however, require five minutes of yelling to quieten down. Mrs P. knows they are not inspired by her class—and why should they be? Music doesn't pay the bills, not in Greece anyway, and if you're looking for a ticket out of here, you're better off getting an engineering degree and immigrating to the Netherlands than learning to play the trombone.

"No, no, no—flutes, you're out of tempo!"

The entire orchestra is now glaring at the flutes, and more specifically at Stella.

"Need I remind you we have a concert in two

weeks?" Mrs P. snaps.

Stella goes red and hides behind her brown, lanky hair. "Sorry," she mumbles as the orchestra resumes playing.

Ten minutes into rehearsal St. Roman gets bored. He tampers with the metronome, confusing everyone as the tempo goes from turtle slow to lightning fast. He opens the window wide so that a draft blows everyone's sheet music and they have to spend ten minutes putting the pages back in order. When Mrs P. dismisses the class everyone is tired and irritable except for St. Roman, who hums the concerto's leitmotif as he takes Alex's sheet music out of his bag and hides it under the piano stool.

The school gym is empty now but for Stella practising her part on the flute, again and again. St. Roman feels for her. Wasn't he, too, once ridiculed for not being as talented as his peers? He wasn't the most talented singer when he was a young deacon in Constantinople. One day he sang the psalms so poorly that he was asked to step down, while the clergy laughed at him.

But then, that same night, the Virgin Mary came to him in a dream. She handed him a scroll and ordered him to eat it, and because it was a dream Roman did as he was told. He woke up in the middle of the night, sweating and feverish, and began composing.

Stella abandons her flute and walks up to the piano. Someone's left his sheet music under the stool, the

Mozart concerto. Stella looks at the notes and hums the soprano's part. She stands up straight, breathes through her diaphragm, and starts to sing.

Stella's song is like a scarf blown away by the wind; it swirls up towards the ceiling and St. Roman jumps up to catch it, but then the scarf turns into a bird-in-flight and soars above the gymnastics bars and towards the school gym's ceiling. St. Roman watches, enchanted, as the bird explodes into a dozen butterflies at the moment the aria reaches its peak. And now the butterflies are snowflakes, falling softly around Stella as the song comes to an end.

St. Roman smiles, remembering his own triumph when the hymns he had composed were sung at mass for the first time. It must be a miracle, the clergy whispered in wonder, for who could have expected that a young deacon who couldn't sing would write music so divine? And on the other side of the gym's half-open door Alex leans stunned against the wall, his lost sheet music forgotten.

*

"Everyone please take your seats so that the concert can begin," the school principal says at the microphone two weeks later. "Today our school celebrates the feast day of St. Roman the Melodist, patron of our neighbourhood church. And before I give the stage to our school's orchestra, let us remember St. Roman's life and contribution to church music."

Backstage, Stella is trying not to panic as the theatre

fills with parents and students. Part of her wishes she could go back to the days when she was third flute, and Mrs P. was yelling at her instead of making her sing in front of the entire school. The school principal drones on about St Roman and the miraculous scroll, but Stella isn't listening. She prefers to think of St. Roman as a boy bullied by his peers who decided one day to do something about it. If that's not a miracle, she doesn't know what is.

*

Lida Papasokrati *grew up in Athens and studied medicine at the Université Catholique de Louvain in Belgium. She has been a member of the Brussels Writers' Circle since 2015 and a member of the Geneva Writers' Group since 2016. She won the 2nd prize for fiction at the Geneva Writers' Group Literary Awards, and her work has appeared in the anthology* Offshoots 14: Writing from Geneva.

David Ellard

The Future Ain't What It Used To Be

David Ellard invites you to feel his pain at the direction modern science fiction has taken

WHEN I WAS A CHILD growing up in the seventies, the future, as related by the Star Trek series, looked good. Two hundred years hence, the Cold Warring nations of the world would bury their differences, form a Federation and launch Captain Kirk on his five-year mission to boldly go where no man had gone before.

The women of the future, at least the ones on the Starship Enterprise, boldly going where presumably no woman had gone before either, looked good too. They performed a variety of subordinate, if not downright pointless, functions on board while wearing the shortest of mini-dresses.

It seems to me now looking back on it all that Lieutenant Uhuru was probably ripe for a spot of downsizing. Her "job" was to listen to messages through a pair of strange-looking earphones and then repeat them to the Captain. Why didn't they simply cut out the middlewoman, save some space on the bridge and relay the messages directly through the tannoy?

And then there was the one with the extraordinary Ukrainian-peasant-meets-beehive-style haircut—Yeoman Randy, was it?—who hovered round the bridge holding a clipboard, a task she was barely able to perform due to quivering so much with scarcely controlled lust for the good Captain.

All of which was as it should be.

But then the nineties and Next Generation arrived, and it turned out that, a bit further on in the future from Captain Kirk's voyages, the ultra-short dresses get traded in for unisex lycra trouser suits—admittedly of a bondage-grade tightness—and some of the women on board attain executive grade.

And what jobs they have. Take for instance—and her title says it all—"Counsellor" Deanna Troy. She takes any opportunity to use her special powers—not so much telepathy as tele-empathy—to commune with passing aliens, understand their motivations, their psychological issues and generally feel their pain.

Excuse me, but whatever happened to the spirit of the frontier, to the Manifest Destiny? What happened to the days when a place on the Starship Enterprise was a ticket to roving the universe, meeting strange and fascinating new species, and zapping them?

I'll tell you what happened. Post-colonial revisionism has gotten hold of our science fiction series and it won't let go.

It's not just Star Trek, look at the progression from the original Star Wars movie to the follow-up trilogy. In the 1976 original, the enemy are the Stormtroopers who, under all that fancy shmancy white body armour, are people—flesh and blood. Human beings who end up getting massacred by Luke Skywalker and his cohorts. The whole thing is an absolute bloodbath, the death toll easily reaching double figures half an hour into the film.

But for the (2001) return flick, The Phantom Menace, the Jedi fodder are no longer people, but pathetic gangly-looking robots called "droids". The destruction of these droids is wholesale but strangely uninvolving. I mean where's the fun in mashing up crap little robots? They don't **bleed**.

It seems to me somehow that it's no longer quite acceptable for celluloid science fiction heroes to carry out wanton slaughter of other human, or even humanoid, beings.

All of which makes me hanker for the moral certainties of creatures such as the Daleks. At least with a Dalek you know where you stand. Its mission in life is to exterminate anything it meets that isn't a Dalek. You can't see Dalek historians extemporising about how regrettable it was that they wiped out a bunch of aliens called "Redindians" on the planet "Northamerica" and what, in retrospect, a cultural loss to the universe that was and how it must have played havoc with the local ecosystem.

Daleks don't feel people's pain; they inflict it. It's a

simple perspective, admittedly open to moral examination, but it does have the great advantages of clarity and consistency.

Actually, it's not so much that I worry about the consequences of our current touchy-feely feel-good science fiction on **present-day** Earthlings. No, it's more the fate of our future descendants that bothers me.

One day humanity may be faced with a gigantic Dalek battlefleet warping out of hyperspace headed straight for Earth with all guns blazing. I just hope that, come the day, we won't get sidetracked from manning the laser cannons into trying to understand the Daleks' problems and speculating as to whether their pathological hatred of other lifeforms might be a result of lack of nurturing in their early species evolution combined with a repressed Oedipal complex over killing their own creator Davros in 'Doctor Who and the Genesis of the Daleks'.

I mean, it's a dog-eat-dog cosmos out there.

*

David Ellard, citizen of Britain, denizen of Brussels, has written poetry, short stories and is now working on a second draft of what he describes as "an epic work of science fiction with erotic elements like Frank Herbert's Dune with a liberal dash of French pornographic thriller Baise-moi.

Alex Dampney

Dressing a wound

The other day, some years ago
I fell and hurt my knee.
A great big gash became a hole
as deep as I could see.

I didn't know a cut could go
so deep into my flesh.
I felt it slice right to my soul
and cleave it from the rest.

The agony was so acute
I screamed then yelled and cried.
Tears streaming down my face,
stomach crumpled up inside.

I found a dressing, big and round
designed to do the job.
I slapped it on the wound and sighed
swallowing my sob.

I couldn't run as I did before
to hop and skip was hard
but no more harm befell my knee
hid safe beneath its guard.

'Though this was all some years ago
the plaster sits there still.
Now a part of me, its glue
has welded to my skin.

Julia's Song

I went with you that sunny day
and castles grew from sand.
Tempting crabs with mussel shells
you took me by the hand.

But then the rain began to fall,
heavy summer thunder.
You said we had to find a roof,
some shelter to hide under.

You picked a house behind the dunes
along the hidden trail.
Ivy covered walls and tower,
the setting for a fairy tale.

Our laughs were loud, we raced full-tilt,
tripping at the door.
Entwined we tumbled at the step,
our bodies crumpled on the floor.

I looked into your face, but then
a cloud obscured your eyes.
You carried me into a world
you'd wrapped in secrecy and lies.

You set the rules. I'd had my fun
at the pier and beach.
Your turn came next. You got to choose
the games you longed to teach.

My cries echoed in those empty rooms,
no-one to mind our games.
So convenient, it seemed to me
you might have organised the rain.

When you were done, you laid your head
upon my chest and cried.
My story ends as autumn falls,
my castle's smashed, the crabs have died.

*

Alex Dampney is an English native who has been
living and writing in Belgium for the last 25 years.
She writes poems and short stories in the tradition
of fairy stories which can be taken at face value
or as metaphors for events that life can throw at us.

Océan Smets

She Kissed My Soul

She kissed my soul while silence was sleeping. She preserved me from the shadows. She did not steal my secrets when I undressed.

She joined me under the stars of my cosmos bed, dared confide her secrets in my ear.

We left for a travel to nowhere. She embroidered with silken words tracks on the air waves. I followed these paths, lands away. She then rested. Her breath slowed. She looked inside me.

I took refuge in ourselves, this warm and humid place where I collected her thoughts. There I got stronger, could erase the material limits, and made abstraction of a wrong body.

I am the Dragon

SHE KEEPS STARING at me, not yet ready to leave her comfort zone, or to meet the unknown, the different. Does she pity me? Does she really long for me?

I am the Dragon. Neither the frog nor the Princess. I am aware of the infinite distance within myself.

Dragons are told, since they are born, to scare, to produce fire. I cannot. So I couldn't get a job in no man's land. Nobody wants a steam dragon as a pet, or so they said.

I have always loved little humans, frogs share with me deep conversations, castles keep amazing books that I have read many times.

"Drag! She screamed in my nightmares, "Help me!"

One misty dawn she arrived unexpectedly.

"Drag, come home!" she whispered in my ear.

She hugged my neck, and we flew away to hers, where people look as though they are happy.

All her room was decorated with dragon motives. It felt cosy. I recall it smelling like my mum's.

But no more. A real Prince came riding by, not long ago, and they left together.

"But you don't know the end of the story. They had arguments every day. One morning the Prince quit her—to think about them—he told her. When he finally came back, one week later, the Princess had left with a dragon".

"Really?"

"You have your own distinctive style, Drag: muscle mass, good manners. You are attractive, intriguing... You're perfect! I will never ask you if you've got fire, you don't need it", explained Unicorn.

I Think I Will

1) "I THINK I WILL…"
WALK the beach of Accra again, collecting shells
PAINT baobabs and African houses
DIVE the icy waves of the North Sea
SWIM in the tranquil Mediterranean, jump her waves and dive till her sand
FALL in love for a Muse, who will cuddle me in stormy nights
DANCE immersed in sensuality
WRITE haikai and kanjis, tales and dreams
READ all the books to touch their words
KISS women, babies, and massive trees
FORGIVE all those who once hurt me
BE ABLE to find my own path leading to my own story

*

Océan Smets *is a published author of poems, flash fiction and nonfiction. He is the 2015 winner of the Spanish 1st International poetry competition Writing Verses, the 2014 winner of the First Literary Contest of Short Tales for Train Travelers by Thalys in Kemkem, Argentina. His poem "Feuille de Route" was published in Verses from the Heart in 2013 in Spain. He is currently working on his second social sci-fi novel.*

Martin Jones

Shimmer

TWENTY-FIVE MILES to the southwest of Moscow is a large expanse of low, thickly wooded hills. In the hot summers, it is cool under its green canopy. Apart from the rare report of a hunter's rifle sending a flurry of crows, like ashes, into the heavens, all is silence. In winter, the snow lies thick on the ground, and the trees stand out starkly against the white sky. A river, the Klyazma, runs through the hills. On the banks of the river there is a remote village, half a dozen or so peasant cottages. It is called Perelygino.

A mile or so from the cottages, hidden in the depths of the woods, is a dacha. A bare earth track runs up to its boundary, marked by an ancient wooden fence, and leads onto a driveway, its surface cracked and broken and almost totally overgrown with brambles and birch saplings.

Beyond the driveway is the dacha itself. Once owned by a bourgeois Russian family who had had it built to escape from the gritty heat of the Moscow summer. After the revolution it had been appropriated to the greater glory of the working masses and reserved for the use of favoured party functionaries.

The older trees and younger saplings crowded around the house, cutting out all but a few shafts of sunlight, giving the place an air of gloomy abandonment. A steeply angled roof extended to the front to form a veranda. The door sagged on its hinges, the windows were broken, paint peeled off to expose weathered grey timber. The remains of an old flowerbed, choked with weed, were still discernible. The dacha was singular in one respect. A cellar had been dug into the hard earth. It had been used to store wine. And not just any wine. The finest French vintages. Soviet bureaucrats had developed refined tastes when the dacha was in its heyday.

The wine had been long drunk, and the cellar was empty. Except for a shabby metal trunk pushed against one wall, lid buckled, and hinges snapped. Inside were mouldering bundles of papers, now inhabited by a family of mice. But there was also a dirty cloth package, about twelve inches by eight, bound with string.

*

The man was wearing a heavy sheepskin coat and fur hat, a rifle slung over his shoulder. He strode forward with the air of someone sure of his destination. The ground was thick with snow, which had crusted the branches of the pine trees and piled itself up on them so that they bent under its weight. Occasionally an overladen branch would bend too far, and a great mass of snow would tumble silently to the ground. The man's heavy boots crackled as they scrunched through the surface ice.

He reached the boundary fence and paused for a moment as if to check that the place was uninhabited. He moved cautiously towards the dacha until he reached the door. He tried to push it open. It was locked or frozen shut. He put his shoulder against it and shoved. With a splintering sound that reverberated through the stillness, it burst open. The windows were shuttered, but by the light from the doorway, he could see that the room was bare apart from a large iron stove, rusting against one wall. He stepped inside and stamped his feet to get the snow off his boots. He shook himself like a dog, and fine particles of ice flew off him in a spray. His eyes flickered around the room, then narrowed when he saw the hatchway let into the floor. Drawing a heavy hunting knife, he tried to lever it open. He leant on it, using all his weight and just when it seemed the knife was sure to snap, the door gave way a little. He pulled off his gloves and thrust his fingers into the crack. With a powerful heave, he wrenched it open. Dropping to his knees, he peered warily into the darkness, sniffing like an animal anticipating danger. Apparently satisfied, he pulled a thick stub of candle from his pocket, lit it with a brass cigarette lighter and gingerly made his way down the stairs.

At the bottom he squinted about in the undulating light of the candle. Hot wax ran down its sides and onto his hand, but he didn't notice. The earth walls sparkled with ice, and it was so cold it was painful to breathe. With a grunt of satisfaction, the man knelt by the trunk. It opened easily enough. His hand reached in eagerly, wavered for a heartbeat. He glanced backwards over his shoulder and clumsily crossed himself. With something approaching reverence he lifted out the package and slit the string with his knife. He began to laugh, a strange barking sound that echoed into the stillness.

*

An old, battered Mercedes was parked on the dirt road. The man pulled open the door and placed the package on the passenger seat. He climbed in, lit a cigarette and smiled with satisfaction. He thrust the key into the ignition, but the engine didn't turn over. Swearing below his breath he let out the brake and let the car roll downhill until it coughed into life. He drove towards the city. From time to time, his hand would stray onto the package beside him, reassuring himself it was still there.

*

The hotel had been built in the sixties, and not refurbished since. There was a lot of chrome, and the walls were papered in garish shades of green and orange. The carpet was threadbare in places and the air of shabbiness extended to the staff.

The man went to the reception desk. The receptionist looked at him sullenly.

'I have an appointment to see Mr Smith.'

'The Englishman?'

The man nodded.

She checked the register. 'Room 602.' She pointed towards the lift and then sank back in her chair as if exhausted by the effort.

'Thank you,' he said.

The corridor of the sixth floor was long, narrow and dimly lit. Both sides were lined with doors, once white. Room 602 was at the far end. He rapped on the door. Almost at once it was jerked open. Standing there was a man of late middle-age, tall and slight, with sandy hair and pale blue eyes behind thick glasses. He was innocuous in corduroy trousers, a check shirt and sleeveless jumper.

'So Kaganovich, you're here,' he said sharply. 'You'd better come in.'

He stood aside, but before closing the door, he leant out, his eyes sweeping the corridor.

The room was hot and stuffy. It was clean but utilitarian. A cheap wardrobe, a washstand, table and twin beds. The walls were bare, but the large window overlooked a wintry, nebulous Moscow skyline.

Kaganovich's lips drew back into a taut smile. 'So, you call yourself Smith for this trip?'

'I have a passport that says so.'

'That's convenient.' He tugged out a packet of

cigarettes, lit one, made a preparatory cough, then inhaled deeply. 'And the jewel box. You got a good price? It was a fine example.'

The man calling himself Smith gestured noncommittally. 'Good enough.' He regarded his visitor: pasty, pockmarked complexion, badly cut black hair, someone to be wary of. 'You have something for me?' His voice was brittle.

Kaganovich planted himself on one of the beds. 'Yes. But perhaps a drink first. We are old friends, after all.'

'If you insist. Vodka?'

'Do you have Scotch?' he asked with a sly smile.

With an air of irritation, the man rummaged through a suitcase and produced a bottle and half-filled a glass, grimy with toothpaste.

Still standing, he said, 'So what do you have?'

'Look for yourself.' From the depths of his sheepskin, Kaganovich pulled out a grubby cloth package.

It was surprisingly heavy. Smith unwrapped it carefully. Between the folds of cloth was a mirror in an elaborately cast brass frame. He took it to the window to examine it more closely.

'An icon frame. Shame the icon is missing. Looks 18th Century. There's some writing engraved on the back. I can't read it. It's not Russian.'

'It is Georgian.'

'Is it? Well, it might be worth something if I can get it out of the country. What do you want for it?'

'Ah, but that's not all,' grinned Kaganovich. From his wallet he took out an old press clipping. 'Look at this.'

The clipping was creased and yellow with age. There was no writing, just a photograph and a date, October 1937.The picture was of a stocky man with thick brushed-back hair and a heavy moustache. He was sitting at a desk and looking directly at the camera. The cast of the pale eyes was slightly oriental. Even in the old faded photograph, there was something cold and predatory about them.

'It's Stalin,' said Smith.

'Look at the desk. What do you see?'

Smith scrutinized the picture. The hands were resting on a pile of papers beside an elaborate ormolu inkstand. Instinctively Smith estimated its worth. Then his eye was drawn to something else. A mirror in a heavy frame. He looked from the photograph to the object in his hand. There was certainly a close resemblance.

'You see it?' said Kaganovich.

Despite himself, Smith felt a small tremor of excitement. Expression impassive, he said, 'Are you trying to tell me this belonged to Stalin? If you are, I need more evidence than an old photograph.'

'Naturally.' Kaganovich was emollient. 'The engraving on the back. It says, 'A gift from the Baku Tractor Co-operative to Joseph Vissarionovich Djugashvili.''

'Stalin. Where did you get it?'

'When the great Vozhd died, his servants stole some of his things as mementos. I heard a rumour, and it proved to be true.'

'Go on.'

The Russian shrugged. 'These servants were little more than superstitious peasants. Even in death, they were frightened of him. This one lost his nerve, hid it away. On his death bed he told his wife. It was supposed to be her pension. The widow was too frail to collect it herself so, out of charity, I agreed to help her.'

'Charity?'

'Why not? I am a man of hidden depths.'

Smith couched the lie with a smile. 'I believe you.'

Kaganovich manufactured a modest expression which didn't spread to his eyes, became businesslike. 'So. The mirror. You're interested?'

'Well, if it is genuinely Stalin's then it has a certain market value. What do you want for it?'

Kaganovich mentioned a sum.

Smith pursed his lips. 'Alright. But I'll need more proof. Leave it with me. I know someone who might be able to verify it. It might take a few days.'

Kaganovich thought for a moment. 'Very well. I'll be back at the end of the week. Make sure you have the money. In dollars.'

He stood up and made for the door.

'I'll need the photograph.'

Kaganovich smiled.' I think I'll keep it for the

moment. As insurance.'

Smith propped the mirror on the table. He regarded his reflection thoughtfully. If it was genuine, he knew of collectors who would pay handsomely for it. If it was genuine. He had been doing this for too long to take anything at face value. Going to the window and looking over the snow-covered rooftops he had an unaccustomed sense of unease. I'm getting too old for this. Perhaps I'll make this my last trip.

He dialled a number on the telephone. It was answered swiftly. 'It's me. I have something. Tomorrow? Good.' He replaced the receiver in its cradle.

I need a drink, Smith thought, and the thought surprised him. He was not really a drinker. He couldn't afford to be. With the people he dealt with it paid to be alert, in control. But once in a while won't hurt, he said to himself. He pulled on an ancient tweed jacket and made for the door. He glanced towards the mirror. The surface seemed to shimmer as if made of mercury. He looked more closely. All he saw was his own face. The pale apparition disconcerted him. Have I aged that much?

The hotel bar had its usual clientele of businessmen, policemen, trying to look inconspicuous in ill-fitting suits, prostitutes. The room was bathed in a blue fluorescent light, imparting on the faces of the customers the grey tinge of old rags, transforming eyes into dark pits. He felt reckless and had several drinks in rapid succession. A prostitute, very young, approached him, but he curtly waved her away. As a general rule, he wasn't very fond of women.

He was beginning to feel very drunk. Too drunk. He levered himself away from the bar and weaved his way towards the lift, brushing against a policeman who curled his lip contemptuously. He got to his room, fell on the bed and was instantly unconscious.

*

He awoke next morning, his temples throbbing. Automatically he leant towards the bedside table. A shiver of anxiety ran through him. His hand fluttered over the surface, searching. When he found his glasses, he sighed with relief. Ever since he had been a child and his eyesight had begun to fail, he had felt a terror of blindness, of being plunged into darkness. He looked at his watch and groaned. Breakfast? His stomach heaved at the prospect. No time anyway. Hauling himself out of bed, he dressed hastily. Re-wrapping the mirror, he thrust it into a leather attaché case. At the door, he turned back. He had dimly registered that something about the room was changed. It was the other bed. The sheets were disordered or crumpled on the floor as if someone had spent a restless night. That's odd, he thought, before a wave of nausea swept speculation from his mind.

After the stuffy heat of the hotel, the cold on the street bit at his face. He sucked in the frosty air and felt better. He decided to go through the park to clear his head.

It was almost deserted, and he walked briskly through the trees, avoiding the icy pathways. For no apparent reason he felt an impulse to glance behind him. A huddled figure, strangely indistinct, was hurrying after him. He stood still, waiting for the figure to approach, but despite its efforts to catch up, it remained at the same distance. Smith was disturbed. It must be the vodka last night. I should know better than to drink that stuff. God knows where it came from. He turned on his heel and moved on quickly, fixing his eyes at the park exit. Looking back again, the figure was still there, and the distance between them appeared the same. He trotted on, faster now, but when he turned back the figure was still there, still hurrying, still the same distance away. Smith felt a tremor of irrational fear. Now he was running, breath coming in harsh gasps. He ran to the park gates and spun around. There was no-one there. He could feel a film of sweat freezing on his brow.

He took a deep breath. Calm yourself. It was nothing. Just your imagination. But despite himself, he felt badly frightened. Over the road, he saw his tram. Dashing across the road, and nearly being run over, he jumped on board just as it was pulling away.

Peering through the grime on the rear window there was no sign of his pursuer. He sat down. This is definitely my last trip.

*

The tram was crowded, the air thick with the smell of

wet wool and cabbage. The other passengers were anonymous, sharing the same pallor and dishevelled appearance. He anxiously scanned the streets through the condensation soaked window. He was headed for Lyubertsy, a worker's suburb in a part of the city he didn't know well. Moving from the city centre, the landscape changed and became a wasteland dotted with apartment buildings with scarred doors and seamed with rusty drainpipes, balconies weeping stains.

He pushed his way off the tram. The pavement was icy, and he almost slipped. He felt old suddenly, unsteady on his feet. He hoped this was the right stop. His destination was hard to miss. Four towering apartment blocks all grimly identical, capped with snow like man-made mountains. They housed thousands of people and amongst them was the apartment of his, well, hardly friend, colleague. Basil Antanov, a retired professor from the Surikov Art Institute, supplemented his tiny state pension selling his knowledge of Russian works of art. Conveniently, he couldn't afford to be too discriminating about who he did business with. A steel floor plan screwed to a concrete pillar showed him he needed the tenth floor of the farthest block. He hurried across the bleak square. He looked back once anxiously, but there was no indistinct figure hurrying after him, threading a way between the smashed bottles and discarded paper cartons.

The small lift rattled erratically upwards until it stopped with a shudder. The steel grate was stiff, and he needed to wrench it open. Out on the open walkway, the wind cut through him, and tears sprang into his eyes. There was a breath-taking view over the snow-covered city until it dissolved into a distant haze. He found the flat and the door was opened by a young girl of eight or nine. She said nothing but stood aside and pointed to an open doorway at the end of the narrow corridor. Nodding his thanks, he went in. It was stifling hot.

The room was a bedroom and it smelt of the mothball smell of old people. Propped up in bed was a frail old man with a meagre grey beard. His eyes were dark and intelligent.

'So, Mr Smith, you have something to show me.'

Wordlessly Smith pulled the package from the bag. The old man unbound it tenderly. He hefted it in his hands and turned it over to look at the back. From somewhere beneath the bedclothes he produced a jeweller's glass and examined it minutely. When he read the inscription, he gave a sucking noise through his teeth.

'Where did you get this? What do you know about it?'

Smith told him all he needed to know, no more.

'I think everything you have been told is true,'

For the first time Smith allowed himself a frisson of excitement.

'It's certainly 17th Century, maybe a little older. It's provincial work, not of the very highest quality but still very fine. It's probably Georgian. The inscription on the back certainly is, but more recent. You know what it means of course.'

'And the mirror. Is it modern?'

'You see the surface. 'The old man held it to the light. 'The surface is uneven. It shimmers.'

'Yes, I noticed that before.'

'It's not new, at least a hundred years old.'

'Thank you. That's what I needed to know.'

'You think it's his?'

'Yes.'

The old man laughed wheezily. 'You know there's an old Georgian myth that if someone is reflected in a mirror their soul is trapped inside.'

Despite himself, Smith felt his stomach flutter. 'No, I didn't.'

The old man handed it back, a cat presenting its owner with a dead mouse. 'Just hope it's not true then. I wouldn't want to spend the night with the spirit of Comrade Stalin.'

*

Back in his hotel room Smith felt utterly drained. He lifted the mirror from his attaché case, paused for a heartbeat, then thrust it back, buckling up the straps. Going to the wardrobe, he placed it carefully on the bottom and shut the door. It was dark by now, and he turned off the lights and lay back on the bed. He tried to sleep. He had just dozed off when he heard a rustling sound. Switching on the light nothing happened. He glanced out of the window; the outside world was shrouded in darkness.

'Another of those damned power cuts.' Smith muttered to himself. But he was an experienced traveller. Edging across the room to his case he fumbled inside and brought out a torch. As he did so something brushed against his leg. He stifled a cry of alarm and snapped on the torch. The beam swept the room, caught the mirror and was reflected back. Everything seemed in order, but he felt a creeping sense of unease. He tried to shrug it off. This is ridiculous, nothing but childish imaginings. But he couldn't bear to turn the torch off and leave himself in darkness. Wedging it into the side of the bed so that it threw a pool of light above him, he gazed at it, almost hypnotised. Gradually his eyelids began to droop. He had a vision, startling in its clarity, of a wide dark expanse and in the middle a lonely figure, stooped forward as if gasping for breath. There was something so desolate about the image he opened his eyes and lay staring at the pale circle on the darkened ceiling. When he closed them again the same image reappeared. It began to roll on, as if it was a jerky old film. Then the image changed. A dark figure with outstretched arms was running through a moonlit wood. The face turned as if to look directly at him. Smith gasped in horror. The eyes were pale and slanting and glowed with malice. He had seen those eyes before. But the most horrifying feature was the mouth. It gaped and shut convulsively like some mindless deep-sea predator. The teeth were blackened and when they snapped together they clashed as if of iron. Smith tried to jerk upright, filled with inexpressible dread, but couldn't move. He was paralysed. Horror clutched at his heart. His eyes began to close involuntarily. Uselessly he fought to keep them open. The images continued to replay themselves, but now rolled on. He saw the man glance over his shoulder, give a start of terror and flee, desperately. He came to a wall, scrambled over, fell, scrabbled to his feet and ran on. Smith's eyes sprang open again. He was gasping for breath, too, as waves of cold panic swept through him. Again his eyes inexorably shut, and the film replayed itself, the pursuing figure now in sight. Again and again the process repeated itself, Smith fighting to keep his eyes open, and losing, the man growing more exhausted, stumbling, the creature gaining ground. Smith was now almost crazed with fear, his skull felt as if it was full of molten metal. His chest felt like it was about to burst apart as it heaved with wracking sobs. Then from somewhere deep inside him came a notion that if he stopped fighting it, saw it through to the end, then he could rest. Almost immediately he felt himself relax as he surrendered. The images repeated themselves, but now they were getting closer. The man was caught, he began to scream and for the first time Smith saw his face.

*

Kaganovitch was the one who found him the next morning, on the bed, arms trying spastically to push away some unseen object. His thumbs were bloody and his face caked rusty brown. His empty eye sockets were clotted and congealed with something Kaganovitch couldn't recognise. The other bed was in total disorder, sheets stained, the pillow torn. Glancing around the room, he saw the mirror, shimmering in the pale light from the window. He bared strong, yellow teeth. He won't need that any more, he thought, and thrust it beneath the folds of his sheepskin.

*

Martin Jones lives in Brussels with his wife and children. He is the author of award-winning short stories and flash fiction. He has written two novellas, a feature-length screenplay and is currently working on his second novel, a thriller set in Malta in the 1930s. www.martinrjones.co.uk

Claire Davenport

What is the Capacity for Love after This?

What is the capacity for love after this?
Bitter powder, chemical chowder,
from brain to heart to brain you flit,
butterfly turned drone clunking louder.

Little girl blue recovers treacly heart, eponymous love.
Come to my writhing hands reaching for rows of cheeks,
even you gangly loudmouth with so much poison to prove.
Come with your odour, brush lips from which silky love leaks.

Hurry and let resurrected hands excoriate your pain.
Let me point out the colours, the stars, let's kiss.
Suck me dry before I hit so-called sane.
And what is the capacity for love after this?

What's What

This waitress knows what's what,
a beer glass she sets down.
Suddenly meek eyes seeing my lot,
fallen dog and dense bone.

You took me to that office,
at the back never seen.
Me the wavering novice,
and you the cat, cream.

You entered a body not your own,
spitting words by quaking tongue,
needling in wretched wire, now sown.
Any need now to speak of this, that rung?

So this waitress shuns a weary paying hand,
in a vow of silence, no why, no what.
Bloodshot eyes reading a person canned.
Seeing well, I'd say, clean of scheme, plot.

For I don't think you know what's what!
You, the faux crusader, quickly a villain through.
But see here now, you've been caught!
For beer and tender dethrone Judas in you.

Acts of God

We are just an act of God.
Anything other than that'd be 'odd.'
Xylophonic heels herald our coming,
dutifully prancing, such golden-ratio plumbing.

Managers deign, 'jobs a god 'un',
but not as good as that of unborn son.
Rooms of eyes tire as we talk,
but alight at hips in switching walk.

"Did you go run last night my boy?"
"Yes sir," two new friends overjoyed.
Me too says girl in ambient tune,
(And faster than phantom brothers impune).

I am an act of God.
Faster than you, old sod.
Nothing but a serendipitous divination.
Apologies the overactive imagination.

Wiling away the hours in this office,
Fathers, brothers, husbands love us.
Xylophonic heels herald our coming,
prancing around, such golden-ratio plumbing.

*

Claire Davenport is a writer living in Brussels. She has been widely published as an EU correspondent in a past life, and some of her work landed in publications such as More Intelligent Life, Wall Street Journal, BBC and the Guardian. These days she is working on screenplays, one of which was recently shortlisted in a contest. She is part of a screenwriting collective, Punchdog Productions, and is working on a novel which explores the lot of Irish women living under Catholic dogma.

Genevieve Shapiro

Santa's Bells

THE LOOK ON WEE MRS. MCMURTRY'S FACE when she opened the door and saw the young couple standing on her porch was a mixture of horror and hospitality. Frank Sinatra's silky *Christmas Waltz* floated out into the cold evening air. Her son had finally come home for the holidays, and she should have been thrilled. In fact, she *had* been thrilled when he'd told her he would make it this year. And she'd been over the moon when he'd added that he was bringing his girlfriend, whom his parents had never met. But he had omitted to mention that his girlfriend was a zombie. Her skin was paper-white. Her eyes were icy pale. She looked beautifully dead.

After a brief but telling gape at her, Mrs. McMurtry stepped forward. "Darling, it's good to see you," she said, and threw her arms up around Joe's neck, disregarding the snow that had collected on his shoulders and scarf. Then she turned to look into those icy white eyes. "Hello. You must be Kelly," she said, and gulped.

"Lovely to meet you, ma'am," said Kelly, and held out her hand with a smile.

Joe's mother shrank back before remembering her manners. Then she smoothed her red sweater over her skinny frame, and with a deep breath and a strained smile, she shook Kelly's hand.

"Come on, let's go inside," said Joe, with an apologetic look at his girlfriend and drew both women indoors. "I think I smell eggnog! My mom makes the best eggnog coffee." He was almost gabbling as he bent down to undo his boot laces.

Kelly unwound the scarf from around her neck and looked around. Behind her, Mrs. M. was hissing questions at Joe, and Kelly overheard the Z word. The entry hall was cozy and bright with jackets and scarves on hooks, and a red mug of steaming coffee which Mrs. M. had left on the bureau. Kelly sniffed appreciatively. She adored the smell of coffee, even though she hadn't been able to properly taste it since becoming a zombie.

The arch leading to the next room was decorated with garlands of silver tinsel and tiny bouquets of jingle bells. Kelly gave one of them a shake, and Mrs. M. turned from Joe at the sound. This time her smile wasn't forced. "Do you like those, dear?"

"They're beautiful," said Kelly. "When I was a little girl, every time I heard them, I would run to the window and look up into the sky, hoping to see Santa Claus."

"Yes, me too!" said Mrs. M, her eyes shining. "Only I always believed that when you heard Santa's sleigh bells, you could make a wish and it would come true."

"Mom always goes all out on Christmas," said Joe, seeing the opening they needed for a convivial evening. "She's a magician with the decorations."

"Come in and see for yourselves," said Mrs. M, who seemed more at ease now. She picked up her mug and ushered them into the living room.

It was a bonanza of silver and red garlands twining around lamp stands and table legs. Twinkling rainbows of lights looped cheerfully along the tops of the tall bookshelves and peeked out from the leaves of large potted plants. A YouTube video of a fireplace crackled cozily from the big screen in front of the sofa, upon which a cat lay curled up beneath a reindeer Afghan. A fat little evergreen next to the kitchen door boasted blue and green lights, magically bubbling ornaments, and hundreds of glass balls and painted birds.

"Darling!" called Mrs M. "They're here! Come out and say hello!"

Joe's father appeared in the doorway with a tray of cookies in his mitted hand. He was a big man in an apron, and he wore a chef's hat with a sprig of mistletoe pinned to it.

"Hello kids!" he boomed, coming towards them. He set the tray of cookies on the table, and there was a waft of ginger and cloves. He engulfed Joe in a bearhug, then turned to Kelly.

"Kelly, is it? Grand to meet you!" He swept her into a warm hug. No one saw her look of surprise because her face was buried in his apron, but when he released her, she was smiling happily.

"Guys, you have to try these cookies to make sure they're ok for the big party. It's a new recipe I got off Yummly, and you never know with that site."

"Now Ian, I don't know if she—" said Mrs. M. "I mean, don't you eat—?"

Everyone looked at Kelly, who sighed. "Brains?" she said. "Yes. I'm afraid I do eat brains."

"Rats," said Mr M. "I thought I had bought everything I needed, but I haven't got any brains."

"That's ok," said Kelly. "I do eat other food. And I love cookies." And she reached for a gingerbread square. The cookies were golden brown, soft and springy, and each had a cinnamon dot in the center. They were good, but not as spicy as the gingerbread of her childhood. Something about being a zombie had altered her ability to taste subtle flavors. As a result, she'd started eating spicier foods and drinking ever stronger alcohol. She missed flavors. "Oh, do I detect lemon too?" She lied.

"You got it!" said Mr. M. "You tasted the secret ingredient!"

"See, mom?" said Joe. "It's not so bad being a zombie." He put his arm around Kelly's waist and grinned at his dad. "Hey, maybe if I eat some brains, too, I'll pass the Bar this time." They both laughed.

"Come on, let's have a coffee before everyone else gets here," said Mrs. M. "I take mine with vanilla and eggnog. Would you like yours with?" She looked dubiously at Kelly. "What do—"

"Whisky," said Kelly.

"Attagirl!" roared Mr. M., and clapped her on the back, then went to the liquor cabinet.

They got their drinks and arranged themselves around the cat, who didn't budge.

"Cute cat," said Kelly. "It's very quiet."

"It's dead," said Joe.

"Asleep, dear, he's asleep," his mother said. She tucked the blanket under one stiff paw

"Eternally," said Mr. M., and clinked his mug against Kelly's. "Chin-chin."

Joe turned to Kelly. "If he were alive, that cat would be older than me. Mom had him taxidermied after he died of old age."

That's when the lights went out.

"Whoops," came Mr. M.'s deep voice. "My deep-fryer must have overloaded the circuits again. I was making—"

There was a silvery ringing from the front hallway. Then the jingle bells settled into stillness.

"Make a wish, everyone!" whispered Mrs. M., and for a moment, no one spoke.

Then there was a creaking sound as Mr. M hauled himself out of his recliner. "Well, I'll go check the fuses," he said.

They heard him fumbling around in the kitchen, and then a series of clicks as the fuse box opened, and he threw various switches. Then light flooded the house, and everyone sighed in relief.

Mr. M. came back into the dining room saying, "Well, so much for the bacon doughnuts. Sorry, Joe, I know those are your favor—"

The words died on his lips, and he stared at Joe. "Son?"

Joe was pale, as pale as the moon, and his eyes had gone an icy white. "That's okay, Dad," he croaked in a voice raw with emotion. "I think I have a new favorite food now."

"Joe?" said his mother faintly. She was staring at him too. "Did you...make a wish?"

"Yes," he said. "I wished to be a zombie. Kelly's very special to me. She's the one, mom. I did it for her!" He turned with tears of joy to his girlfriend and froze.

Her face was pink, her eyes a sparkling green, and she was sipping ecstatically from her mug. She was, very clearly, human.

"Oh god," he said. "Kelly, did you...do that for me?"

She looked up. "Well, for the coffee, really. And for you," she added hastily. "I wanted your parents to like me."

"We did, honey, we liked you," said Joe's dad. "We still do!"

"Yes, dear, of course," said Mrs. M. She set down her mug on a side table and looked at Kelly. "But honestly I'm glad you're no longer a zombie. I never could stand—." She fell silent as she glanced at her son, and realised what she was saying.

Joe turned to glare at her and then started. "Mom!" he cried, and his jaw dropped. Then he turned and glared at his father. "DAD!" he barked.

Mr. M.'s eyes became very wide as he looked at his wife. "Holy cow," he muttered in fascination, and they all turned to look at her.

Mrs. M. looked from one face to another. "What?" she said. "Why are you staring at me?" Her voice trailed off as she realised they were looking not at her face but below it.

She looked down and then shrieked. Her breasts, once a modest size 32A, now strained the red sweater and what must be a size 32EEE bra. They rested on her lap like a couple of puppies, reaching nearly as far out as her knees.

She stood up and slowly backed away. Her boobs followed her.

"Ian!" She whispered. "What have you done?"

"Well, the sleigh-bells...the wish...you know," said Mr. M. apologetically. "You don't mind, do you? I mean, I wouldn't mind if you did the same thing to me." He looked hopefully down at his pants, and then in disappointment looked at his wife.

"Didn't you make a wish, honey?"

"Yes," she answered, crossing her arms to support the strange new load. "Yes, I did."

Near the sofa, there came a light thump as something landed on the floor. And then they all heard it.

"Meow?"

*

Genevieve Shapiro *Genevieve Shapiro draws cartoons www.gentoons.com and writes zombie fiction that refuses to turn out scary, despite her best efforts.*

Klavs Skovsholm

Belle of the Ball

A REAL PALACE *MUST* have a Christmas Ball. At Cygnet Castle this was no different. With its white walls and slim towers that reflected in the mountain lake, the castle was swanlike, and Josephine the Goose could see why His Most Royal Highness the Lion had chosen that name.

Excitement was in the air. A small army of raccoons was already hard at work cleaning the palace from top to bottom to get it ready for the holiday season. Josephine knew that the weaver birds in the nearby village had been busying themselves with new ball gowns. She, too, had ordered a dress in canary yellow which, she hoped, would perfectly match her immaculate snow-white plumage.

But the annual ball was also a source of sorrow for her. Josephine was a poor dancer because of her big orange feet. However, today held special promise as the Court would be presented with its new dancing-master. It was well-known that His Highness the Lion had sent his running ducks all the way to the land of the Dawn to find a suitable candidate. So, more than anyone, Josephine pinned her hopes on the newly arrived Japanese waltzing mouse. She could think of nothing she wanted more than to overcome her ineptness on the dance floor and win the heart of Mr Lieutenant the Swan, who danced with such regal stature. She could barely waddle at the thought of his broad shoulders and long muscular neck.

In general, however, Josephine felt out of place here. Her presence was due to her mother's insistence that her beautiful daughter represent the geese at Court. Her mother must have been one of only a few to believe in the necessity of that role, because Josephine was the only goose at Cygnet Castle—unlike the large number of hens and swans.

The swans-in-waiting were especially mean to her. *But why?* she wondered, *I'm as white as they are, just a little shorter.* More than once a swan had reminded her that a common goose was quite superfluous at Cygnet Castle. All her attempts to make friends with the swans had been in vain. And the hens? She had reluctantly come to the conclusion that *they are just silly hens, so absorbed in their matters that they neither recognise the needs of others, nor the coolness of the swans around them.* Josephine's six months at the castle had been very lonely indeed.

The first lesson with the dancing-master was going to take place in the Grand Hall. Josephine stood at the back, behind all the hens—or rather 'fowl-in-waiting' as they insisted on being addressed at Court in order to be equal to the 'swans-in-waiting'. As was their habit, they entered the hall, in great numbers, to occupy the best places in total disregard of what any other animal, with the possible exception of His Highness, might want. Fortunately, Josephine was tall enough to see what was going on.

Then she saw him: a white mouse with a black-and-white head. He was dressed in a peculiar long gown made of a shiny, light-blue material, depicting what looked to Josephine like flying storks. She thought she heard Lord Steward the Fox whisper something about a kimono and imperial cranes to one of the hens, who quickly spread the word among her fellow fowl-in-waiting. *Kimono? I must have misheard*, Josephine corrected herself. Lord Steward pushed his way to the dancing master, brushing aside the flock of hens with their white-powdered plumage. 'Master Mausu!' He greeted with his foxy grin, and swung his paw elegantly toward the mouse. Josephine noticed that streaks of powder had rubbed off onto one of the sleeves of his blue frock coat.

Then the mouse bowed, and they could all see his tail sticking out of a hole in the back of his curious gown. This immediately created a flurry of activity among the hens, who lowered their heads and spread their wings as wide as they could.

Josephine took a step back at the sight of all the bums suddenly pointing in her direction. When the mouse looked up, Josephine's gaze met his over the backs of the silly hens. He smiled at her. She returned his smile and inclined her head as if she had been a swan. Once more, the mouse nodded elegantly, and Josephine had the impression that his gesture was meant especially for her. The hens followed suit, thus releasing another small cloud of powder.

Josephine sneezed, making the hens turn and look at her, grinning at the sight of her watery eyes and runny nostrils. She sneezed once more. Now the eyes of each and every bird-in-waiting, Lord Steward, and even the dancing-master were gazing at her. She blushed all over, and then she curtseyed and hastily turned around to leave the Grand Hall in search of some fresh air. Behind her, she heard the hens giggle.

On her way down the corridor, she heard music from the Grand Hall. The dance class had started without her! Devastated, she climbed the castle battlements. Wandering around, she felt as if her heart was about to burst. She even thought of throwing herself into the lake. Josephine was so upset she couldn't see that her reflection showed her mother had been right: she was an extraordinarily beautiful goose with her delicate orange beak and exquisite white plumage, more like the silky feathers of an egret than those of a simple goose.

*

One of Josephine's more pleasurable chores at Cygnet Castle was *to sit pretty,* as His Highness called it. She, like all other birds-in-waiting, had to spend hours every week sitting on the sofas in the castle, simply looking pretty. The next morning was such a *sit pretty* morning. Josephine was still sad from the day before, so she made sure she chose her favourite armchair by a window overlooking the lake and the mountains.

She longed for her village beyond the ridges in the distance and was so absorbed in her reveries that she didn't notice Master Mausu until he stood in front of her, bowing at least as deeply as the day before. In fact, she noticed that his wide sleeves were just short of touching the floor.

'Master Mausu, what a pleasant surprise! I am Josephine, the Goose,' she smiled nervously.

'And I am but a mouse here to serve,' he answered, with a sly grin. Josephine giggled. 'Forgive me for interrupting you,' Master Mausu continued, calmly holding her gaze.

'Why, not at all.'

'I was saddened to see you leave my dancing class yesterday.' Josephine blushed but sat still. The mouse's eyes truly looked sad while he said that, she noticed.

'It was the powder. It always makes me sneeze.'

'Don't you use it then?'

'No, but the hens do. Most of them are grey, you see, and only white is pretty to them...'

'In my country only geishas powder that way. If you allow me to say so—you truly are the most exquisite white I've ever seen. Just like the finest of silks.'

'I am still a goose,' Josephine protested softly. 'The swans shun me and make me feel inferior.' Her eyes began to fill with tears.

At this point there were noises behind them. They turned around. Mr Lieutenant the Swan, accompanied by a couple of fierce-looking swan courtiers, came marching through the hall. No one looked at them. Josephine stretched her neck as far as she could to keep the lieutenant in her sight. A teardrop fell from her beak.

'But he stole your heart all the same,' Master Mausu whispered, thinking aloud, while he observed her reaction to the largest of the swans who had just passed them by.

'I beg your pardon?' she said, meeting his gaze again.

'I said, I hope to be able to be of service.'

Josephine nodded.

'Before I leave again.'

'Are you leaving soon?'

'I am. Didn't you know? The Crane Emperor only meant for me to stay a week. I'll return the day after the Christmas Ball when my escort has arrived.'

'How will you get back?'

'On a swan, of course,' he winked. Josephine giggled, again.

'Could you come to my quarters, Josephine, when you are finished with...' he looked uncertain, 'with what you are doing now?'

'*Sitting pretty*, you mean?'

'I want to give you some private lessons. Would you like that?'

'I would be delighted! I'll come as soon as I can!'

Master Mausu turned and left the hall.

Josephine was speechless. Did he just offer to help her with her dancing? Her heart leapt with joy. The next hours at the window seemed never-ending.

*

During the last days before Christmas at Cygnet Castle, Josephine had plenty to do. She had, however, managed a few clandestine lessons with Master Mausu between her *sitting pretty* and other chores. She was happy in Master Mausu's company, but she still felt inadequate dancing. *How am I ever going to manage the ball*? she thought, sadly. She already saw herself relegated to dancing with the donkeys.

Because of their gentler disposition, all birds-in-waiting were expected to decorate a designated room. Josephine had been asked by Lord Steward to take Master Mausu's room under her wings. None of the hens had shown any interest, anyway, as all were set on the rooms of the officers at Cygnet Castle. So, while the dancing master was downstairs toiling with the hens, Josephine busied herself with preparing the room for his return. She had noticed that Master Mausu liked simplicity and order. *So he should appreciate the simple beauty of garlands of ivy*, she thought. In the gardens she picked ivy and a few large white flowers which had not yet been bitten by the frost. Back indoors, she put them with the garlands.

When the music stopped, the sound of the cackling hens leaving the Grand Hall drifted up to the room like a wave. Josephine put the last touches to her work and stepped back. The dark green leaves and the white flowers looked lovely. She was thrilled with the result.

As Master Mausu entered, he stopped in his tracks at the sight of the transformation. He looked at the garlands, at their shiny leaves interspersed with chrysanthemum flowers. Only then did he remember to greet Josephine who, in turn, nodded her head as a swan would do.

'Master Mausu, my task was to decorate your room for Christmas! Do you like it?'

'I'm honoured. After all, I'm but a simple mouse here to serve.'

An awkward silence fell upon them.

Then Master Mausu withdrew a stick from his sleeve. 'Come now. Dance a little for me,' he said, and he swung the stick in the air to show the rhythm. Josephine moved around with no hesitation. In fact, she found it elating to be in the company of Master Mausu.

She turned, twisted, and curtseyed right on the beat, while she imagined dancing in the arms of Mr Lieutenant the Swan. She was so absorbed in her dream she didn't notice that Master Mausu had stopped indicating the beat with his stick and was walking up to her. Josephine jumped. Had she done anything wrong? She met his gaze, but he didn't give away anything of what he was thinking. He never did, she had noticed.

'My dearest Josephine,' he said softly. She took a step back. 'I don't know where you got the idea that you can't dance... No swan in the world can do it better than you.'

'But I'm only a goose.'

'As I said, no swan can do it any better. Never believe otherwise!'

Josephine curtseyed, still not believing her ears.

'I now want to teach you a minuet, which is a favourite of—.' He was interrupted by a commotion outside, where the sky looked as if it were about to start snowing. He turned and ran to the window. Josephine was surprised by the agitation of the usually poised mouse, so she followed him and looked over his shoulder.

There, on the lake, they saw the staircase which descended from the castle into the water, and nine large water birds swimming in a wedge formation towards it. Their leader was in the front. Josephine couldn't believe her eyes. These creatures looked like swans, but couldn't possibly be! They were all black!

'Who are they?' she asked.

'Swans of the Imperial Guard. The Crane Emperor has seen fit to send some of his personal guards to escort me back to the land of the Dawn after the ball.'

'But they're black, Master Mausu!'

'Yes, Josephine, black like ninjas.'

'Like ninjas?'

'Come! We must go and greet them!'

Master Mausu offered no further explanation but turned and headed to the door.

At the top of the staircase leading to the lake, an icy wind greeted them. Snow was clearly coming soon. They noticed that Lord Steward, Mr Lieutenant and several other swan courtiers were already at the bottom of the stairs, and that the hens had filled its entire upper part. Master Mausu was not one to push his way through, so he and Josephine slowly descended the stairs as the hens reluctantly, but respectfully, let them pass.

Josephine watched Lord Steward welcome the imperial swans and present Mr Lieutenant and the other courtiers to their guests. She couldn't hear what Lord Steward said, but could see the black swans were bowing repeatedly. For their part, the white swans stuck to the usual measured nodding of their heads.

Her heart constricted with longing at the sight of Mr Lieutenant, but she stayed right behind Master Mausu, afraid that the hens would cut her off. Eyes sent her daggers from all sides as she brushed against powdered feathers. She kept her head low, fixing her eyes on the back of the mouse as they approached the bottom of the steps. With every little step she took, the hens jealously filled the space that opened up just behind her, and she felt as if water was rushing against her. The hustle and bustle around her almost made her trip, so she put her feet down with great care.

When they were near the bottom of the stairs, Master Mausu suddenly stopped and straightened up. Josephine almost bumped into him. She stood firm and pushed her broad back against the curious hens. The powder in the air made her eyes run, but she managed not to sneeze.

Then the leading black swan broke away from Lord Steward and the white swans and swiftly stepped forward.

'Mausu-san!' he exclaimed.

The mouse bowed so deeply that his tail went skywards and Josephine worried that, this time, he might knock his head on the stone steps.

She was suddenly struck by the splendour of the black swan, whom she could now see up close. She had never seen a broader breast or a more muscular neck. His feathers were as dark as a moonless night, and his beak and feet were fiery red. Not even Mr Lieutenant the Swan could provoke such emotion in her.

'Hakucho-san! I am honoured and delighted to see you, old friend,' the mouse said.

'The honour is all mine, Mausu-san.'

'Captain, may I present to you Josephine, the Goose,' the mouse said, as he stepped aside. 'Josephine, may I present you to Master Hakucho, Captain of the Guard of the Crane Emperor.'

The black swan just stared at her, seemingly overwhelmed by her beauty.

At that moment the ice-cold wind picked up and swept down from the mountains and across the lake, bringing with it snowflakes, some of which landed on Josephine. The ice crystals glittered in her white feathers.

'Josephine-san,' the black swan said, holding her gaze. 'Mother Nature smiles at us by making the fairest of snow geese sparkle.'

Josephine was speechless. She turned red and was utterly confused. For a moment she just stood there. Then she lowered her head and curtseyed like a goose would do.

'Fairest of snow geese?' the hens around her muttered under their breath.

'Captain, I'm just a common goose. I thank you, but—'

'Gentlemen,' Lord Steward said loudly, interrupting Josephine. 'Please come with me so I can show you to your quarters.'

He went up the steps so rapidly that the hens jumped aside to make room, landing on top of one another. Meanwhile, all the swans, as well as Master Mausu and Josephine, followed Lord Steward into the castle.

Behind them the snow began to fall densely and, over the next hours, the temperature dropped dramatically. Winter had come just in time for the Christmas Ball.

*

The following day, Josephine was due for another *sitting pretty* after her lesson with Master Mausu. As she slowly made her way through the palace, she studied the festive transformation which the palace had undergone over the last couple of days. Every room was now decorated for Christmas with colourful ribbons and holly.

Through a door left ajar, she peaked into the Grand Hall. In every corner giant Christmas trees had been put up, which the squirrels were busy decorating with red ribbons, and pine cones painted in a variety of shiny colours. *Delightful*, Josephine thought. She also noticed a small bandstand and, with its back to the fireplace, a big gilded chair with a blue seat where His Highness would hold court that evening. She held her breath, admiring the squirrels fearlessly fitting candles in the crystal chandeliers under the high ceilings. Looking at them up-there made her dizzy. Just then a foot-badger came forth and slammed the door shut right in front of her beak.

Thanks to her classes with Master Mausu, she felt less anxious about the ball that same evening. Strangely enough, that morning he had insisted that she learn a minuet the Crane Emperor and Empress held in high esteem. She didn't see the point as no one else at Cygnet Castle would know that dance, but she had indulged him. Now she felt sure that, should the occasion arise, she could dance the minuet of the

Crane Emperor and Empress without any flaw.

Josephine had the feeling she was being watched as she made her way to her window chair. She could hear no other footsteps than her own, but, whenever she stole a quick glance over her shoulder, she had the fleeting impression that a dark shadow had just moved out of sight. She started to waddle faster, then abruptly stopped to listen again. *Was there a sound?* she wondered. *I must be making things up,* she told herself. Then she reached her chair.

What she saw took her breath away. The lake had frozen overnight, and virgin snow glittered under the icy-blue, sunny skies. Once again, she turned and looked around. She couldn't shake off that eerie feeling of being watched.

*

That evening Josephine put on her canary-yellow dress for the ball. The weaver birds had done a great job! There was a lot of excitement within the walls of Cygnet Castle, and tension had been steadily rising since the King's arrival on a Unicorn-drawn sleigh.

Happily, and with light feet, she lifted up her skirts and carefully descended the winding stairs from her small room under the eaves. At a window in the staircase she paused briefly to look across the courtyard into the Grand Hall. In the soft light of hundreds of candles, the massive Christmas trees looked magical through the tall windows.

In anticipation of His Highness's imminent arrival,

birds-in-waiting and courtiers in red gala uniforms were hurrying into the Grand Hall to greet him. Josephine squeezed in behind the long rows of powdered and perfumed fowl, all dressed in vivid colours.

Then trumpets started to play, announcing the arrival of His Most Royal Highness the Lion. He emerged through the large doors with his regally feline gait, accompanied by the Lord Steward and several courtiers, including Mr Lieutenant the Swan. All the fowl and the other feathered and furred creatures bowed in reverence to their King. As soon as he had taken his seat, Lord Steward gestured to Master Mausu on the bandstand to start the orchestra playing. The dancing began.

Josephine stood with her back towards the wall and took it all in. Hens and swans were dancing merrily with the courtiers in their shining red jackets. Master Mausu conducted the orchestra, but Josephine couldn't see any of the imperial swans in the hall, as she had expected. How odd! Mr Lieutenant the Swan stood next to Lord Steward and close to His Highness's chair. Josephine tried repeatedly to catch his eye but to no avail. She mused that her worries might be founded, and her heart sank. Already five dances had passed, and not a single courtier had invited her to dance.

Then the fifth dance came to an end. It was the moment Josephine had been waiting for. As was the tradition at Cygnet Castle, after the fifth dance of the evening it was for the birds-in-waiting to choose a partner. And the prettiest of them all would be granted a wish by their King! The excitement rose. Everybody coyly eyed the courtiers before they got into action.

This is my moment! Josephine thought as she started to waddle all the way across the hall in the direction of the King. Some hens noticed, thinking she might ask His Highness for a dance. It caused a stir and silenced all the guests.

Josephine noticed the King's kind face as he caught sight of her in her yellow dress. Lord Steward looked on stiffly, but Mr Lieutenant the Swan resolutely turned his head away from her as she stopped a few paces away from him. His Majesty turned with surprise to his Lieutenant, but before he could say anything, the foot-badgers swung open the large doors to the Hall, and the imperial swans came marching in. The Captain led them up to the King, whom they greeted in unison.

The King's face lit up in a broad smile at the sight of the black swans, while Josephine looked up at Hakucho, who stood next to her with the rest of his swans behind him. The Hall was silent; everybody was uncertain how to react to this turn of events.

Then the orchestra started to play again. It was a simple, beautiful tune unknown at previous balls at Cygnet Castle. Josephine recognized it immediately as the minuet of the Crane Emperor and Empress. Hakucho turned to Josephine, bowed, and his swans stepped back to create space in the middle of the dance floor. He took the first steps, stretching his neck and beak towards the ceiling while opening his wings. Josephine copied him, and they slowly began to circle gracefully around each other.

Hakucho had eyes only for Josephine. She felt dizzy, not only from the constant circling, but notably from the presence of the most beautiful swan she had ever seen. Her feet trembled, but they didn't let her down. She looked fleetingly at Mr Lieutenant. When she met Hakucho's loving gaze again, her heart overflowed with love for him. She almost stumbled at that moment.

'My fairest snow goose,' he whispered as they stepped up close and turned holding each other's glance. 'Come with us when we leave tomorrow morning before sunrise. Please! Come with me. Otherwise, I shall have to leave my heart behind.' Josephine was jubilant hearing those words but also frightened by the prospect of leaving all behind herself.

She wanted to cry out and tell each and every one about her new-found love, but she held back because she feared the scorn of the swans. The music stopped, and Josephine and the Captain of the Imperial Guards stopped too, looking at each other, slightly out of breath. There was complete silence in the Hall.

Then the Lion King rose from his chair. He applauded and bowed ever so slightly to Josephine and Hakucho. Now all the fowl and swans curtseyed to reflect the

King's behaviour.

'Josephine the Goose,' the King said in his deep voice. 'You are the Belle of the Ball! And as tradition bids, on Christmas Eve the prettiest bird is entitled to make a wish to her King. Come, Josephine, and make your wish!'

Josephine felt as if the Hall was spinning. She stepped forward and curtseyed deeply before the King. 'Sire...' she began uncertainly. She stole another quick glance at Hakucho and made up her mind: 'Sire, I wish to accompany Master Mausu and Master Hakucho when they leave tomorrow morning.' There it was. She had said it!

'Consider your Christmas wish granted, Josephine, the Goose!' the King said. He burst out in laughter and called for more wine. Master Mausu grinned and swung his stick to start the orchestra on a merry tune and, within moments, everybody was dancing again.

*

Early the next morning, before the sun had risen over the mountains and while everybody else was still asleep, Josephine was on the frozen lake with Master Mausu, Hakucho and the eight Imperial swans. They took off in perfect formation. The Captain was in the front, while Master Mausu, in a small travel basket attached to two swans, was in the rear. Josephine flew close to the basket to keep Master Mausu company.

They circled a few times around the towers of the castle to gain height before they made for the ridges.

The sun's rays were just starting to appear. And so it happened that, on a clear Christmas morning, Josephine took off with Master Mausu, her new love and the Imperial swans to seek her fortune anew, in the land of the Dawn. `

*

Klavs Skovsholm lives in Brussels. He is the author of two short historical novels, Golden Fields and At the Bay. His illustrated children's book Die Kokerboom in Afrikaans and isiXhosa was published in cooperation with the South African Stigting vir Bemagtiging deur Afrikaans and he co-authored an illustrated children's book Bogen for Småfolk, both published in 2017, see www.sbafrikaans.co.za and www.jambo-schule.dk

T.D. Arkenberg

Aftershock

"War destroyed the Grand Place but saved the Town Hall."

The blaring sound of the dismissal bell prevented Sabine from further explanation.

Damn! She thought as her pupils bolted for the door. The bombardment of Brussels couldn't compete with a sunny, late September afternoon. She'd have to clarify her meaning at the beginning of the next session or risk leaving her students with the impression that Louis XIV's artillery destroyed Brussels in the name of building preservation.

Sabine hated it when she couldn't get through her lesson plan. Instead of the full, vibrant, picture she strove so hard to draw, she left her students with mere fragments of history. With increasing frequency, disciplinary matters stole her instruction time. Even when she didn't have her hands full of refereeing arguments between pupils, she found her authority questioned or worse, dismissed by eleven and twelve-year-old boys. They didn't always verbalize their prejudices, but the rage that flashed in their eyes was unmistakable.

It had been three months, one of the last days of the previous school year, since a rather painful outburst. The boy, baby-faced Mehdi, embarrassed her in front of the entire class. "What makes you think you can teach?" he shouted after she corrected his claim that Belgium would never have a Queen. "You're just a stupid woman."

Sabine tried to push the words from her mind. She had the entire summer to bolster her self-confidence. Two weeks at the Belgian coast in August helped, despite the gray skies, crowded sidewalks and overpriced meals. Erik had been a real sweetheart too, letting her sleep late and offering light massages as she lay on a chaise longue on the beach. She should have figured that things were going too well. He became argumentative late in their holiday, an afternoon of too much beer and self-pity over returning to an overbearing boss and a dead-end job. She'd grown used to Erik's increasing sullenness, but his verbal abuse was something new.

Sabine began her fourth year at Sint Albert, a primary school that offered instruction in Flemish, nagged by her own frustrations. She mentally readied herself for the new year with a vow not to let the little darlings, as she called them, get under her skin. She owed it to the good kids, the ones who wanted to learn. And there were plenty of them. Even though their voices were often drowned out by the bullies. *Merely childish rhetoric*, she repeated to herself. *Could happen anywhere.* If only she believed that. She was sinking into a deep despair, a feeling of profound isolation. Not only at school, but in her adopted city, and, if she were honest even at home with Erik.

Sabine was born and educated in Ghent. Her parents weren't happy when she decided to move to Brussels. "It's dirty, unsafe," they said. "And to think it was once a Flemish city." Her mom and dad were good people, but they also had their prejudices. Simple, working-class people, they didn't venture beyond their close circle of family and friends, mostly white, Catholic and, proudly, Flemish. Her parents' small world was immune to the demographic changes taking place across Belgium. They didn't object to the social evolution; they simply didn't want any part of it. Sabine wasn't interested in that kind of life. A university degree had exposed her to sophistication and diversity.

"If you must take that job, why don't you commute?" That was her mother's last-ditch effort to keep her daughter anchored in Flanders.

Sabine didn't want to waste her life sitting in Belgian traffic. Strong bonds that kept people tethered to families and childhood friends were often given as explanations for the country's notoriously long commutes and clogged motorways. Perhaps the traffic was merely a convenient excuse. In truth, Sabine wanted to escape her clan.

Sabine was determined. Her partner Erik, a boy she had known since primary school, snagged an entry-level position with the European Commission. "If I play my cards right and avoid a murder conviction or drug-smuggling charge, it's a job for life," said Erik with a smirk.

The couple found a cheap, basic apartment just off the Place Saint-Catherine, an area popular with young professionals and tourists. Sabine and Erik embraced the carnival atmosphere that descended upon the square at weekends and dismissed the smattering of vagrants and drunks, drawn by the abundance of bars and cafés, as mere urban color.

The church that gives the square its name never failed to impress Sabine. At night bathed in spotlight, its magnificent stone edifice radiated with an orange-apricot glow, the color of a rich sunset. During their first year or so in Brussels, Erik and Sabine used to sit on a park bench holding hands, taking in the exciting neighborhood and sharing news of their days. In recent months, however, Sabine sought solitary refuge on the bench away from Erik and the simmering stresses of home.

Sabine's parents were right on one account. Despite the daily rounds of street sweepers, Brussels never cleaned up very well. Rubbish littered the gutters while animal waste, missing paving stones, and beggars turned the narrow sidewalks into obstacle courses.

After too many sneers and a chorus of 'I told you so', Sabine stopped inviting her parents for weekend visits.

Initially, Sabine found the predominance of French speakers quaint, even a bit exotic. But as time passed, and frustrations with her job and life mounted, she grew aggravated that most shopkeepers and others she met on the street didn't speak, or even understand, Flemish. "I'm a stranger in my own country," she complained. "It's my capital too, damn it."

With her mind focused on the interrupted lesson of the 1695 Bombardment of Brussels, Sabine hustled down the gray corridor toward the teachers' lounge. Except for a friendly Congolese janitor and a couple of teacher's aides chatting in front of an open classroom, the hall was deserted. The hour after classes were let out for the afternoon had become her favorite part of the workday. She worried she was losing her passion. 'Am I turning into one of those jaded teachers I swore I'd never become'?

"Hello, Sabine," said Hilde, a tall, slender woman with her gray hair pulled back into a bun. The veteran teacher never used makeup. She wore her creases and weathered skin as a badge of honor. "Teachers' faces are like tree rings. Every year brings another wrinkle. You'll see." Hilde provided that counsel to a fresh-faced Sabine on her first day at Sint Albert. As part of an informal mentoring program designed to discourage new teachers from quitting, Hilde took

Sabine under her wing. "Haven't put in your notice today, my dear, have you?"

"Not yet, but the day's not over," Sabine said with a short laugh.

The exchange had become an after-school ritual, a running joke between the two women who had fast become friends. But this afternoon, Sabine's canned retort rang deeper. Her day wasn't over. She had one more appointment, a parents' conference, concerning one of the more persistent rabble-rousers in her class.

Sabine sat at one of the large metal tables in the lounge. The staff had returned from summer break to find their break room painted bright yellow with a border of daisies where the walls met the ceiling. Pastel-colored mugs replaced black, chipped cups. "Something small to lift morale," the Principal, Mr Mickelsen said when welcoming the staff back to school. But all the new paint and colorful china couldn't camouflage the shabbiness of the building, a post-war eyesore of steel, beige brick and grimy glass.

Hilde placed two mugs, pink and robin-egg blue, on the table and took a seat across from the younger woman.

"Rough day?" Hilde asked, blowing over the steaming tea.

Sabine poured milk into her mug without looking at the other woman. "I'll say. Seems I spend more time keeping the peace than teaching. I still don't understand why they can't get along with each other."

"It's cultural. The little monsters hate each other."

"You talking about my people?"

Sabine and Hilde turned toward the deep voice. Youssef, the new mathematics instructor, stood in the doorway. Sabine blushed. She found the tall man, about her age or a bit older, maybe even thirty, very handsome. His dark eyes, hair and skin, couldn't have been more different from her fair Flemish features or those of her partner Erik. The snug, white polo shirt Youssef wore accentuated his exotic features and muscular frame.

"Oh...oh sorry. I, I, d...didn't mean to offend," Sabine stammered.

Hilde threw her a scowl. "Sorry? For telling the truth? Pish posh!" Sabine got the sense that Hilde didn't like Youssef, but it was too early to tell. Proclaiming herself a 'crusty old lesbian', Hilde proudly passed judgment on newcomers to the teaching staff. "They accept me, I accept them. Simple as that," she explained. "Like? Well, that's a different matter altogether."

Youssef laughed. The flash of his brilliant white teeth contrasted with the dark stubble of his neatly trimmed beard. Sabine hadn't noticed before how full his lips were. "No offense taken," he said. "In these skirmishes, I'm on your side. It was the same at my last school. They can be little bastards. I'd pummel them myself if the bruises wouldn't show."

Sabine's blue eyes grew wide; she looked to the

door then back to Youssef, avoiding direct eye contact. "Shh. Mustn't say things like that. Mr Mickelsen doesn't approve."

Hilde rolled her eyes at her young protégée. "The truth hurts, Miss Three-Wrinkles. You'll learn that soon enough," she said, tracing a deep line that creased her cheek from nose to chin. "Care to join us?" Hilde looked up at Youssef and pulled a chair out from the table.

"Sure. Got time for a quick cup before boys' basketball." Youssef walked toward the electric kettle and poured the still-hot water into a glass with a tea bag.

Sabine returned her gaze from the male teacher's athletic backside to find Hilde, her eyebrows lifted, grinning at her. After Sabine had confided in Hilde about troubles with Erik, the older woman had taken up the mantle of matchmaker. Batting her hand at the other woman, Sabine felt embarrassed and worse, foolish. Youssef wasn't her type, at least she didn't think so. Her parents wouldn't approve, not that she cared. Or did she? It wasn't prejudice. She simply always imagined herself settling down with a solid Flemish boy like Erik.

"It'd make all of our lives much easier if you could convince your... people to get along," Hilde said to Youssef when he joined the two women at the table.

"They don't listen to me any more than they do you."

Hilde cleared her throat. "Ahem, you are a man."

Youssef nodded. "True. But even that doesn't make a difference in the struggle between Turks and Moroccans."

"What are you?" Sabine said, instantly regretting her forwardness. "Oh, so sorry. You don't have to answer that. Forget I asked." She felt her cheeks warm.

He smiled; his eyes crinkled at the corners. "Let's see. I'm a football fanatic who's addicted to hamburgers, *pommes frites* and *Chimay Bleu*. I'm a jazz lover, a cat owner, a Scorpio… and yes, a Belgian of Moroccan descent."

"Scorpio, huh?" Hilde said. "Got the looks for it. That's for sure." She winked at Youssef. "Now you're both blushing. That's good. Now no-one's at a disadvantage."

Youssef regained his composure. "I don't mind you asking. Both my grandfathers immigrated here in the sixties, from the same village and worked in the coal mines. My parents were born in Charleroi. And yes, before you ask, theirs was an arranged marriage."

"But you're single?" Hilde asked with a mischievous grin.

Youssef nodded. "No prospects I'm afraid. Can't impress the ladies on a teacher's salary."

Sabine glanced up at the clock shaped like a full-rayed sun, a new addition to the room. "Oh, my. Gotta run. Parents' conference for one of my little… darlings."

*

"What's for dinner?"

Sabine shook her head. She hadn't even taken the key out of the front door to the apartment. "And a good evening to you too, darling Erik." She shut the door and placed the plastic grocery bags from Carrefour onto the kitchen table. "How about leeks and carrots? I've been mending too many popped buttons." *He deserves the jab about his ballooning weight,* she thought.

"Very funny." Erik came up behind her and kissed the nape of her neck. "I'm sorry, honey. How was your day?"

"Chicken, green beans and potatoes." Her voice was cold, monotone.

"Huh? Oh, come on. I said I was sorry."

Keeping her back to him, Sabine merely shrugged.

"Tell me. I'm interested, really I am."

Sabine dropped a bag of potatoes on the table with a thud and turned toward Erik. "Horrible. It's only week three, and I'm ready to surrender. The kids are out of control. Their parents aren't much better."

Erik squeezed her shoulders. "Sit down. Let me pour you some wine."

"What about din—"

"Relax. Dinner can wait."

Erik helped Sabine out of her light-blue raincoat. He guided her to a soft chair in the living room. She heard the dull pop of a cork and the clanking of glass before he returned with a tumbler of white wine. He sat on the sofa opposite and lifted a blue can of beer from the side table. From the stale smell of his breath and his glassy stare, it wasn't his first.

Gazing at his face, she pictured him with a beard. "Ever try *Chimay Bleu*?"

A puzzled look flashed across his clean-shaven face and was gone in an instant. "Too expensive, bitter. Now, tell me about your day."

Sabine shared her frustrations about her meeting with the parents: always the same story, mothers who came alone, fathers who couldn't be bothered no matter how flexible she was with the proposed timeslot.

"At least Hamed's mother was honest. She earns points there."

Erik sat forward. "What did she say?"

"'Hamed's father thinks the boy would do better with a male teacher,' she said. "Can you imagine? That's where the kids get this shit."

"Sorry, honey. That's fucked up. I wish you didn't work there."

"But I do, and I can't quit." She looked into Erik's eyes, red and puffy from too much alcohol. "May as well get used to it."

Erik wriggled back into the cushions; he dropped his chin. "Guess this is the wrong time to bring up our freaky neighbors."

Sabine rolled her eyes to the ceiling before reclining

her head. She offered a sigh of surrender. She'd grown tired of Erik's wild stories. He'd become convinced that the two brothers, Middle Eastern by language and appearance, were terrorists. Sabine dismissed his suspicions as xenophobia, too much beer, and an overactive imagination.

She forbade him from sharing his suspicions with her parents. "That's all they need." She imagined being dragged back to Ghent by her hysterical mother and judgmental father. So far, Sabine had managed to keep Erik from calling the police. School and Erik's increased drinking and mood swings were stressful enough. She didn't want to introduce even more strife into her life by waging war with the neighbors.

"I'm serious, honey. Don't you want to hear about what I saw today?"

Sabine sat up and groaned. After taking a large gulp of wine, she glared across at her partner. She had no time for his nonsense. "No! I'm sorry, but I have to deal with these people every day while you traipse off to the Commission. Least you can do is to put up with a little neighborly irritation. This is Brussels for God's sake. May as well get used to it."

*

Months passed; the school term ended. Sabine checked herself out in the bedroom mirror, pleased with her reflection. She looked radiant for the final day of the school year and her very last day at Sint Albert. She was wearing a new black dress with a white blazer from Zara, and her blonde hair was done up in a short, chic, summer cut. She added her silver and lapis earrings and matching pendant for good luck. They were a Valentine's Day gift... from Youssef.

Have the last nine months been a dream? Her life had undergone a stunning transformation. Besides exchanging Erik for Youssef, she had landed a job at the prestigious International School in Boitsfort beginning later that fall. She and Youssef agreed that he'd continue at Sint Albert until she established herself at the new school. He was in no rush to leave Sint Albert. He was encouraged that his afternoon basketball program was bridging the cultural divide between the feuding factions of boys. She and Youssef planned to use the summer break to find an apartment on the nicer side of town: Ixelles, Uccle or maybe even nearer her new job in Boitsfort.

Sabine leaned closer to the mirror. Studying her face, she grinned. There it was, wrinkle number four— her badge of honor. She'd proudly point it out to Hilde who'd begin calling her, Miss Four-Wrinkles.

Sabine practically floated toward the tram stop in her new shoes. It was a beautiful June morning, even by Brussels standards. Looking to the horizon, she grinned at the memory of her interrupted lesson at the beginning of the school year. Atop the Town Hall, the gilded statue of Michael the Archangel, the city's patron saint, gleamed in the morning sun.

At the sight of the school building, Sabine's stomach

knotted. *A mix of excitement and good-bye jitters, that's all,* she thought. An idling lawnmower sat unattended in the building's small front garden. Careless, she thought as she mounted the stone steps to the entrance, especially with small children expected within the half hour. Inside, she glanced toward the administration office opposite the front door. Perhaps I should report the lawnmower? But Mr Mickelsen's vigilant secretary wasn't at her post. The spinster with a permanent frown was usually perched at her desk like an old barn owl, keeping tabs on the comings and goings of staff.

Things seemed odd, upended. The two corridors leading from the front vestibule were deserted. Normally, a few teachers shuttled between classrooms. Even Mr Finch, a steadfast creature of habit with whom Sabine exchanged a daily morning greeting, wasn't at his desk eating crackers and reading The Times of London.

"This isn't the weekend or a holiday?" she muttered to herself. No, the doors would be locked. There was also the idling lawnmower.

She gasped. That's it! Sabine guessed that the school staff was gathered in the lounge. A surprise! Her co-workers intended to surprise her on her last day. They'd send her forth from Sint Albert with well wishes and cake. Hadn't Youssef hinted as much the prior night? With a mischievous smile, and saying he had "things to do," he left right after dinner and spent the night at his apartment.

Sabine hastened her step till she approached the teachers' lounge. Hushed voices floated out the open door into the corridor. Her ears perked; her feet froze. Are those sobs? When she entered the doorway, her eyes took in the colorful streamers and balloons. A large cake with "Congratulations Sabine" sat in the middle of the table around which Hilde and others huddled.

Hilde looked up. Instead of returning Sabine's broad grin, the older woman appeared frightened, sad—her face gray. After rising from her chair, Hilde took Sabine's hand. "You haven't heard, have you, my dear?"

Sabine felt all eyes turn to her. "Heard what?"

"There's been an explosion... in the Metro."

"Damn terrorists again," someone else muttered.

Sabine's heart sank for the innocents. For surely there were victims. Madmen always unleashed their fury to maximize the carnage. "Oh my God, no. Where?"

"Louiza."

Sabine was shocked but not surprised. Louiza was an ideal target. It was the Metro station below Tiffany, Dior, Versace and dozens of other luxury boutiques that lined the Gulden-Vlieslaan and Louizalaan.

Hilde pulled Sabine into a firm embrace. "There's more my dear girl." Over Hilde's shoulder, Sabine noticed Fredrik. The slight, rodent-faced science teacher looked ill, his face white. He could barely steady the coffee mug in his shaking hands. Sabine drew back and looked at Hilde. The older woman's eyes welled with tears. "I'm so sorry," she said, "so very sorry."

"Tell me, Hilde. What's happened?"

Sobs intensified among the other teachers and staff in the lounge. Sabine didn't remember much else or how she got back home.

*

Later that night, Sabine was alone in her apartment. She wanted—no, needed—the solitude. Hilde and Mr Mickelsen left only after she insisted they go home to get some rest. Sabine pleaded with her parents to drive back to Ghent without her. They were obstinate, relenting only after she agreed to consider moving back to Ghent even if only for the summer.

Clutching to her heaving chest the pendant that Youssef had given her, Sabine curled up on the couch and sobbed. The day's events kept invading her thoughts. Was it her imagination or did she already know what happened before Hilde quelled her sobs to share the news?

Youssef had been killed. Although authorities weren't releasing any names, there was no doubt. Fredrik's account confirmed as much. He and Youssef had ridden the Metro together, bumping into each other at Kunst-Wet, three stops before Louiza.

"Youssef was so excited about your last day," Fredrik told her between stammering apologies. "He couldn't stop grinning. He'd bought a gift but forgot flowers. He remembered the florist inside the Louiza station. 'I'll hop off,' he said. 'Buy the biggest bouquet of roses and jump onto the next train.'"

The next Metro never left the platform. Two brothers, suicide bombers, blew up the train and the entire station.

*

T. D. Arkenberg is the author of three novels. His work has been honored by, Independent Publishers, Next Generation Indie Book Awards, National Indie Excellence Awards, and ScreenCraft Awards. 'Aftershock' was a Finalist in the 2016 Faulkner-Wisdom literary contest. T.D. is a graduate of Northwestern University and the University of Chicago. www.TDArkenberg.com

Paul Speight

Talking About Death

It's always hard to choose the words.
Hands wring, tongues trip over verbs.
Harder still to know when to stop -
takes time for the penny to drop,
to hold that normal, human, urge
to suggest, to compare, to merge.

To paint their grieving and sadness
onto our own, personal canvas
is natural. But that projection
removes layers of protection.
Can give the bereaved another cut,
Opens doors they'd rather keep shut.

Death may be the great universal,
but feelings remain individual.
Crucial thing is to show you care,
Some empathy whilst being there.

Ultra-modern Pentathlon

The noble Olympic baron
Updated the Greek pentathlon
To train the officer classes
And keep them apart from the masses
But it's not that modern anymore
Not how one likes to fight a war
So they set up some committees
That met in glamorous cities
And delivered a smart report
On a virile new five part sport
First event, piloting of drones
Friendly fire in combat zones
Next up, spontaneous jumping
As IEDs get the heart thumping
Then off we go down to the pool
Spot of waterboarding—keep cool!
A quick scramble back to the huts
One bed for three, due to the cuts
Last one has contestants puffing
Through marathon paper shuffling
Gold medals for winners of course
The crowds cheer until they are hoarse
For brave losers a purple heart
Pinned on the biggest body part...

Rivanelle: We Count Our Days by the Length of Our Nights

As a babe in arms we sleep without frights
Dreaming of Morpheus, his soft caress
Our head hits the pillow, out go the lights
We long to stay up but our eyelids press
But soon come our teens with girls to impress
Burn away the candle, nocturnal sights
Dancing and drinking for sexual success,
We count our days by the length of our nights

Then a tired damsel finds a yawning knight
Bedtimes with each other, rapidly blessed
No more city soirées, neons so bright
Midnight maternity, cries that distress
From dawn to daybreak, one long weary mess
Never seen a charter of parent's rights
Bottle or bottom, wake and try to guess
We count our days by the length of our nights

Then one fine morning when the time is right
Rise our needy swallows and fly the nest
We enjoy the quiet but muse on their flight
Time on our hands, strange new concept called rest
But our hair turns silver, need to sleep less
Message is clear, make hay whilst we still might

We'll slumber enough when we last confess
We count our days by the length of our nights

Prince! Like death and taxes, sleep can oppress
All must obey its call, from king to mite
Rhythms our lives in failure and success
We count our days by the length of our nights

*

Paul Speight is a father, lawyer, bureaucrat and writer. He used to write for Douglas Adam's website, H2G2, when it was owned by the BBC. Now he is working on a post-apocalyptic comedy, and producing poetry and other short works in his spare moments, which are mainly on trams.

Barbara Mariani

Photographic

IT WAS EARLY SUNDAY MORNING when the phone rang.

I was sleeping deeply after a late night out with Sergio. We had made small hours strolling through Roman ruins and sipping wine in *Trastevere*.

The bedroom was already stifling from the summer heat, and I felt slightly dazed and slow. I grabbed lazily the phone on the bedside table. Aunt Renata's number was displayed on the screen. An unusual time for making a call, I thought. I pulled myself up and sat on the edge of the bed.

"Hi, did I wake you up?"

"Yes, you did. Never mind. What happened?"

"Your mother is very ill. You'd better come home today."

She didn't add any further details.

I was taken aback and too numb to ask anything in particular. I said to her that I would leave at once and hung up abruptly.

I turned to Sergio, who was in bed beside me. He was fully awake and was observing me.

"It's about my mother. She's not well. I need to go."

He took my hand "Do you want me to come with you?"

"It is better that I go alone."

"As you wish. I'm free. I have no plans for today."

"I can deal with it. Besides, it doesn't seem a good occasion to introduce you to my family." I let go of his hand and stood up.

I chose mechanically what to wear and quickly packed a bag for a couple of days. I didn't know how long I would stay away, but I didn't want to waste too much time packing. I knew my mother was waiting for me.

"You can stay at my place if you want, you don't need to leave right now," I told Sergio.

"Thanks. I think I will stay here then. It will make me feel closer to you. When are you coming back?"

"I have no idea."

"Let me know; I'll be waiting."

"It's so annoying that just when my mother needs me most, I'm in bed with a man."

"You shouldn't feel guilty."

"Sorry. I didn't mean to be rude."

Sergio and I had been dating for two months. I had mentioned my mother's illness to him briefly, but I had not wanted to make things heavy right at the start of our relationship. He hadn't insisted on knowing. We had left the subject aside.

He accompanied me to the door. We kissed

goodbye, and I left.

*

As I drove past the busy Rome ring and into the countryside, I became absorbed in all kinds of thoughts about me and my mother. I felt uneasy and couldn't wait to be close to her. My mouth was so dry that I emptied a half-litre of water in one gulp.

It was a two-hour drive to my mother's place. She lived in a small town in Marche, where I was born. All her four sisters lived in the same place. My brother too lived there, with his wife and children.

I had been travelling back and forth for twenty years, since I had moved to Rome to study at the university. As my life in the big city became my new home, trips were less frequent. Except during the last two years, when I went back more often because of my mother.

My memory went back years before, to the day I was first told about her illness. It was seven years earlier. I had taken a day off from work. I was worn-out and wanted some time for myself. It was in the morning. I was still in bed and had just started reading *L'étranger*, by Albert Camus. The first sentence of the book goes: *Aujourd'hui ma mère est morte*.

That same morning, my brother Max rang me. He told me that my mother had been short of breath while walking up the stairs to her room. She had been taken to the hospital, where they had found water in her lungs. I knew that wasn't good news. I also recalled that she had a strange cough the last time she had come to see me in Rome. After a few days, the doctor said there was a malignant lump in her lung. She had never smoked a cigarette in her life. Only a couple of years later, after she seemed to have fully recovered, they found out that the origin of cancer was somewhere else in her body, but it was already at a very late stage.

*

I thought about my last conversation with her. We had spoken over the phone two days earlier, on Friday. She had sounded very weak and sad. Over the last months, she had lost fifteen kilos, and the chemotherapy had become unbearable. I had told her I wanted to spend the weekend with her and wanted to introduce Sergio to her. She had replied she didn't want to meet anybody, least of all a new man in my life. Plus, she was not a nice thing to show, she had said.

I felt that she wanted me to come by for the weekend, though. But I hesitated a few seconds over the phone, and the conversation came quickly to an end. It left me with a heavy heart as if an important thing on her side had been left unsaid.

I regretted that my mother didn't want to meet Sergio. He was a simple and very gentle guy. He was born in 1969, like me. He wasn't the intellectual, well-read sort of type I had always gone for, but he liked good music and travels. And he was handsome.

We met at a staff away-day. We danced to the music

from the '80s and got excited at the same favourite songs. At the end of the evening, when the music stopped, and almost everybody had left, Sergio took my hand and guided me outside, into the garden of the 18th century villa, which had been rented for the staff meeting. It was a warm, starry night and a soft breeze was blowing from the West coast. The smell of the sea reached us. We sat on the grass and started to kiss. It was strangely sweet. Later, he drove me home on his motorbike.

A week after our first meeting, a package was delivered to my office desk. It was accompanied by a small red envelope. The message went: "We talked a lot about this song during our first meeting. Here is one of the best versions ever. I hope to see you again soon. Sergio."

I was a bit disappointed that he hadn't contacted me before. Still, I liked his way of getting in touch, through a gift and a card. It felt so much like being back in the '80s.

I did remember the dance, the kissing and the rest of the evening but I didn't have the faintest memory of having talked about that particular song: *Photographic* by Depeche Mode. When I went back home, I played it several times. Not a love song, but a great dance song, which I had never come across during my teenage days. That same evening I rang to thank him.

*

I thought about how difficult the subject of love had always been between my mother and me. When I was younger, she used to turn icy and irritated whenever I gave her too many details of my relationships. But over the last years, when her illness brought us much closer, I noticed that she had become more sympathetic and caring. She seemed to want to let herself go, and she told me things about her youth and how she had met my father. She had spent most of her teenage years in a girl's boarding school run by nuns, in a small village away from another small village, where her family lived.

Being the first of five daughters, life had been particularly hard for her. She had been given a stricter education and much less freedom than her sisters. She could not buy the dresses she liked or put on make-up. She was not allowed to stroll in the village square on Sunday mornings with boys of her age. She adored dancing but was forbidden by her parents. The only occasions where she could dance were at Carnival or during the patron saint's festival in summer when the entire village gathered in the square. There she danced with her girlfriends and sometimes, when her parents were distracted, she also ventured in a few sways with a boy. My mother was an exotic beauty in a Southern country. She looked like a Scandinavian, tall and slender, with fair skin, long blond hair and emerald eyes.

Those passionate winter and summer nights had warmed her heart and kindled her dreams during the long grey months, spent in a two and a half square metre cold bedroom, in the company of bugs. Her first attempt to read a book was stifled by a spiteful nun, who found a paperback under her mattress and disposed of it. The punishment was cleaning the toilets of her floor for one month. My mother had the strongest and most sincere hate for nuns. Her gentle heart had been frozen right when it was blooming.

When she met my father, she was twenty-three and had just left the boarding school. My father was twenty years older than her, a journalist in his prime. He was looking for a secretary, and his brother introduced him to my mother, who was the daughter of one of his oldest clients at the bank. It was feeling at first sight. My father was love, fun and freedom. At least for her, at least for a young woman who had never seen and experienced anything in life except village festivals. They got married after only four months. He took her to Milan, Paris, Madrid, Vienna. But luck was not on their side. She lost her first child to a heart disease when the boy was two years old. The doctors said the anomaly was probably the consequence of the measles she had caught when she was pregnant. After the tragedy, my father took to drinking heavily. His mother forced him to leave a beautiful family apartment, which he had renovated to my mother's taste since she didn't want it to be "disgraced" by a child's death. After these two blows, my parents moved to the countryside, in a big house which my father designed himself. But he went into heavy debts, and the banks finally seized the house. We had to move to a smaller one, where we spent a few good years. When my father died in a car accident, my mother was fifty and still in love.

*

I parked the car outside the building where my mother had recently rented a small apartment. I felt exhausted by all the thoughts and memories which had stormed through my head during the journey. In the courtyard I noticed that she had forgotten her scarf on the bike, which was leaning against the wall at the entrance of the building. It was a present I had given her for her birthday in August, the year before. I took it with me.

I rang the bell. The main door opened without an answer. I climbed the stairs frantically up to the second floor. I turned they key in the lock and opened the door.

"Mum, it's me!" I shouted.

A strange silence filled the room. The sun at its zenith entered from the window opposite to the door, I could barely see inside the apartment. The door opened directly into the living room. Then, slowly I began to distinguish the scene. All the family was sitting in a semi-circle in the living room, and they were all staring at me. There was my brother, my mother's four sisters and their husbands. They looked motionless and petrified as if immortalised in a living painting.

"Where is she?" I asked.

Nobody replied, and nobody moved.

I immediately rushed to her bedroom. The bed was empty. Instinctively, I went towards the window, which gave on to the back courtyard. I looked outside. A policeman was talking to the building administrator and was taking notes. Two people were cleaning what looked like a red stain from the concrete.

I kept looking at the scene in a stupor, for what seemed an indefinite lapse of time. Then I realised somebody was standing behind me.

"Where is she?" I asked, without turning around.

"She's no longer here," Renata said.

"Why didn't you tell me on the phone?"

"It was too late, they found her early in the morning. She left this."

It was a photograph that my father had taken forty years earlier, during a summer trip to the Alps. My mother was standing on a rock and looking far away. She was wearing tight, black trousers and a white T-collar woollen pullover. She was a stunning beauty. On the back of the photo, there was a message "*I suffer too much and I'm too tired. This is not me anymore. I'm sorry. 15 June 2008*".

*

The day after, Sergio came from Rome for the funeral.

The ceremony was quickly put together by my mother's sisters in a sort of automated way. My aunt assured me that the priest was a good man and that he knew my mother very well. But his speech was dull and anonymous. It could have been about anybody else's life and death, and certainly not my mother's.

At a certain moment, the priest said with acrimony that my mother "had violated the sacredness of life, but that God would forgive her for what she had done."

I was filled with disgust. I took Sergio's hand and whispered in his ear "Let's go. That's enough".

"Yes, let's go and get some fresh air," he said.

He held my hand tight and led me outside. The sun was shining in a clear blue sky, and the air was light. We sat on a bench in the church courtyard, which opened on a view of the mountains.

"I regret not having had the chance to meet your mother. But I'm sure that there is a lot of her in you. And I can't wait to find out."

We remained silent for a long time, holding our hands and looking both towards an undefined direction ahead of us.

*

Barbara Mariani was born in Italy. Her research on T.S. Eliot' s poem "The Waste Land" was nominated as one of the best literary criticisms of the year at the University of Rome La Sapienza. Barbara writes fiction both in Italian and in English and has written a collection of short stories in English. She is currently working on her first novel.

Jay Harold

Shadows

Shadows shed no sight of Sharp Hill
Bye-bye summer breeze, hello September chill
England seems to be but a faraway faint fantasy
As I count the days and watch the leaves
Around me turn to brown
One by one, falling down
Down
Down, down to the mossy ground
On what must have previously been
A field, mighty, vast and green

Songbirds silent, townsmen too
Skies turn grey and hearts turn blue
Rain drizzles down through the ancient trees
Dark days are due, dogs bark with unease
My vocal cords burn as I howl at the breeze
And England seems to be nothing
But a faraway
Faint
Fantasy

Force Seasons

You are an archeological site
I dig you
A psychological delight
So ambiguous
And after all, your summer hair
Will be my fall and I won't care

You are the study of the bones
You're hip
I'm humerus
But broken
And I will wind up splintered
As you cast a spell of endless winter

You are the delta and the source
Soothe me like a hot spring
Drag me off my course
You are far more interesting
Than my future, this is true
Unless my future is with you

Cornbread and Iced Tea

Perennial pines tower in the Alabama sky
The backyard's once green grass has gone and died
Buster barks, beckoning me with his puppy eyes
Begging me to throw him a bone or a ball

We run down the steps of the redwood deck
And a memory raises the hairs in my neck
Buster barks, frightening me, an infant nervous wreck
But I begin to doubt whether it happened at all

On the front porch, Grandpa smokes a cigar
And drinks Jimmie's iced tea; Grandma gets in the car
Buster barks, he's upset but she's not going far
I pet him, and he wags his tail again

And old freight train choo choos; its sound moves me
    to tears
Jimmie's corn bread tastes godly, and so does my beer
Buster barks, we're closer than we have been in years
I never thought I'd say this, but I miss you, old friend

*

Jay Harold recently earned his MA in Creative Writing from the University of Essex. He is currently working on his first novel and a collection of poems. His blog is: jayharold.blogspot.com

Patrick ten Brink

The Apple

Half an apple, peeled
On the pavement
Round side up

This one is fresh
Today's offering
To passing pedestrians

Skinned with a knife
Judging by the flattened rounds
Of its side

A tangy hemisphere
Freshly sculpted
Clean, still

Last week's half apple
Lay in the same place
Its edges brown

The one a month ago
Fresh too
Initially

The first one
Appeared
9 months ago

Each week a fresh
Half apple, peeled
Round side up

Strange punctuation
Or symbol
Like a repeated beeping
Of slow Morse code
In a language
Unknown, to me

Tempting Angels

White wings spread wide
Half a dozen pairs
Hover shoulder-height
In the ill-lit square

Six angels to be
Hang in the air
Golden haloes waiting for heads
Wings calling for arms

A man, a woman and a child
Curious
Approach

The woman nestles
Under a halo
And laughs
But doesn't fly

I watch as one by one
Try wings
Haloes
I wait
All laugh
No-one flies

Alone, I try the first
I can move the wings of the second
The halo of the third fills my head with song
The fourth is too small
The fifth has sandals
I slip off my shoes
My arms into the wings
Head under halo

My wings twitch, flex
I beat my wings, and
Fly
Above the buildings
Air caressing my face

Down below, five pairs of wings wait
Beside my unlaced black shoes
I laugh and wonder
What other shoes will settle next to mine

Urban Worms

Red, coiled, wide-open mouths
Poking out from pavements
Humanity's creation
Plastic urban worms

They hover
Knee-high
Gaping up
Thirsty
But their mouths
Fill with trash

Others have burrowed back
Into the ground
But are stuck
Held in concrete
Their bodies permanent hoops
For unsuspecting feet

Yesterday
Three more
Copper wires
Stuck out from their throats
Reaching into the air
An electric nervous system
Or telephone lines
Seeking contact

Now
A new green one
Emerges
From the ground
What more
Artificial life
Will we spawn?

The Half-Apple

This story is one response to the mystery of the half apple captured in the earlier poem by the same name.

HALF AN APPLE, peeled, lies on the pavement, rounded side up. It was skinned with a knife, judging by the flat cuts. An abandoned, freshly-sculpted, apple. It looks clean enough to eat. I walk past.

A week later, I wander along the same pavement to the charity bookshop. Another half apple lies in the same place. This one is clean cut too, only one thin sliver of red peel remains. The greenish-white flesh is pale brown in places. I sketch the apple in my notebook and scribble, "Saturday, 11 June. The second apple. In front of the yellow house, number 41."

In the bookshop I focus on the titles of the wall of paperback books, the blue, black, and white spines. I tilt my head left and right, taking in the titles. I remember the apple, and mutter, 'Someone doesn't like their mum's apples.'

'What did you say?' A woman's voice asks from behind me.

'Oh, nothing. Never mind.' I reply, embarrassed that I spoke my thoughts. I smile at the woman sitting behind the counter laden with books. Her eyes are pale grey, a tinge tired. She wears a short grey-black wig. 'I was just reading the titles.'

'I don't think we have a book with that title,' she says as she nudges a pile of books towards a man with a crumpled blue shirt standing on her right. 'Do we, son?'

The man, gaunt, with weary reddish skin and watery light blue eyes, stares at me as he runs his finger along the spines of the pile. 'Nope. Never heard of it. Strange title.'

I smile. 'Never mind. Thank you, though.' I turn back to the shelves.

'What did you say the title was?' asks the man, now standing next to me. I can feel his breath. Coffee and whiskey. Cigarettes. 'I can look out for it, for you.'

'That's very kind, but I'll be fine.' I try not to breathe in.

'Suit yourself. I am here to help, always. We have *Neverwhere*, but not, *Nevermind*.' He swivels away before I can study his face.

He grabs two piles of books from the counter, presses his chin down on top, shuffles to the back of the shop, and disappears into an unlit room. I think he sniffs the books before he put them down.

I quickly pick up a novel and put it on the counter.

'Would you like a brownie or an apple with that?' asks the woman as she punches a code in the cash register.

'Sorry?'

'No extra cost. We're trying to welcome people to our shop.' My hand stretches towards the plate with a stack of square brownies. She leans close and whispers, 'The apples are better for you, you know. An apple a day...'

'Thank you... I'll take the fruit then.'

The bell chimes on the door as I leave, the apple in my right hand. I don't look back, but feel that the woman and her son are watching me.

At home, I flip open my sketchbook, take out a sharp knife and slice an apple in two. I peel it, paring away thin rectangles of skin, one after the other. I hold the first half next to my apple sketches, shake my head and eat it. Crunchy, fresh, delicious. I skin the second apple, peeling away squares. A better fit this time. I lay it on a plate and note the time—10:16.

It takes just over two hours to brown around the edges. 127 minutes to be exact.

The next Saturday, I get up early and stroll along on the opposite pavement to where I usually find the half apple, peeled, round side up.

No apple.

I loiter a bit, tie my shoelace, and sneak a glance at number 41. The net curtains are drawn. The door is closed.

I check a parking meter and wander up again.

Still no apple.

I go to the newsagents at the corner.

Six, seven minutes later, I return. There it is—a half apple, round side up, on the pavement, in front of number 41. Its skin is moist, gleaming.

I take out my tape measure. 57 centimetres from the house, 121 from the road. I sketch the apple.

A girl in a red dress whispers to her mother as they

walk along the other side. 'Don't point,' urges her mother.

'Oh God, they think it's me,' I mutter, snapping closed my sketchbook. I pick up the half apple and drop it into the green metal bin on the corner and continue to the bookshop.

The man with the reddish complexion opens the door as I approach. His fingernails are nicotine yellow. The side of his mouth is slightly wet. 'Today we have pears or cookies, if you buy a book.' I can't discern whether it is pear or apple that nuances his smoker's breath as I push past.

'Thank you. I don't know if I'll find anything to buy today.'

'Still looking for *Never Mind*?' he asks with a gleam in his eye. 'We don't have that book. It doesn't exist. I googled it, you know. I was trying to be helpful. Were you mocking me?!' His voice has an edge.

I take a step back. 'No, no, of course not. I was just-'

He stares at me, frowning.

'I...'

He laughs and pats me on the shoulder. 'Got you!' He sniggers. 'We don't have *Never Mind*, or *Neverwhere*. *Inkheart* came in. I thought of you. Thought you might like it. But someone else wanted it...'

'Thank you,' I said, relieved. 'I'm touched.'

'I'll keep an eye out for you, okay?' He plonks himself into a chair next to the counter, grabs a cookie and leafs through a magazine.

His mother pushes the bowl of fruit towards him.

His eyes, fixed on the upper edge of the magazine, don't budge.

I leaf through the books trying to remember an author's name. I hate it that my mind goes blank when I try to summon up a name. It is like my mind is playing games with me. It doesn't help having two pairs of eyes boring holes in your back. I grab a book of poetry, Pablo Neruda.

'He does a great poem about a waterfall of tomatoes,' says the woman. 'Tomatoes are fruit you know.'

'Have a cookie with that one,' says her son.

'Thank you.' I rush to leave, hearing the woman's voice—'Son, people need to eat fruit. If I'd have listened to my mother, I wouldn't have fallen-'

The door chime cuts off her words.

The space on the pavement in front of Number 41 is empty. It looks odd, wrong.

At home, I slice an apple in two and pare away squares of skin, chewing on each as I sculpt my fruit. Not bad. I eat the other half and head back out.

When no one is around I place my half apple, round side up, where the earlier one had been. Now it looks right.

The next week, there is no half apple left on the pavement. Disappointed, I head to the bookshop.

Today there is no bowl of fruit, no cookies, no woman with the wig, no red-faced son. Just an old man, a little stooped, shuffling about.

'Where are the woman and her son?' I ask him.

'Are you family?'

'No…, but…'

'She's in hospital.'

'I'm sorry.'

'I'll go there later,' said the old man.

'I'll be right back.'

I return with a big bag of green grapes. 'She liked fruit. Wish her well.'

The following week, the pavement is again empty. The red-faced man is behind the counter. He is wearing black jeans and a black shirt. A plate with two halves of an apple lies in front of him. He slices off the red peel in little squares. He catches my eye.

'I'm sorry for your Mother,' I say.

He hands me a half apple, peeled. 'Think of her.'

The next week a half apple, peeled, lies on the pavement in front of number 41.

I place another half apple next to it.

*

Patrick ten Brink *writes fiction first thing in the morning and embraces reality during the rest of the day. In 2018, his short story, 'Amelia Borgiotti', was published by the Coffin Bell Journal and his poem, 'Zen Garden, Kyoto', was one of the seven winners of the Dreamers Creative Writing Haiku Context. He is currently putting the final touches to his fantasy trilogy, The Guardians of the Tides.*

Hamed Mobasser

Doggybag

INT. LAUREN'S APARTMENT LIVING-ROOM—EVENING
In a modern, well lit and neatly furnished apartment,
LAUREN, 26, tall and good looking, and SARAH, 25, a
small, skinny girl with short black hair, are sitting on
the living-room sofa, drinking wine. PUNCH, a midsize
dog, is sitting quietly in front of Lauren.

SARAH: It was the lentils.
LAUREN: He doesn't like lentils?
SARAH: No, he loves them. Wanted to make them but
then got mad 'cos I ate beans for lunch. Two legumes
in one day makes me an ungrateful bitch.
LAUREN: He called you that?
SARAH: He called me worse. Right up to the moment I
threw his PlayStation out the window. Then he cried.
LAUREN: So, it's "done done".
SARAH: I'm even considering leaving London, but for
now I just needed to get out of the City for a while.
The girls clink glasses and take a sip.
SARAH: (CONT'D) *(pets Punch)* He didn't even like

dogs.

LAUREN: Well good riddance then.

SARAH: How about you?

LAUREN: *(giggling)* Oh, there is someone.

SARAH: Ooh. Tell me more.

LAUREN: I dunno. I don't know what it is yet. We'll find out when I get back from this trip. I have to see if Punch approves.

(petting Punch) Anyway, for Punch, so, food twice a day. Noon and evening. Walks three times a day, unless you want to clean poop from the carpet. Help yourself to anything you want, and if you bring someone back, large condoms are in the top drawer, small ones in the bottom.

Sarah looks at Lauren and grins.

LAUREN: (CONT'D) Come on, let me show you the towels.

INT. LAUREN'S APARTMENT ENTRANCE—MORNING

Lauren hands the apartment keys over to Sarah.

LAUREN: Be careful, that's the only pair I have.

She bends down to kiss Punch

Bye-bye baby. Mommy is gonna miss you.

Lauren walks out and closes the door. Sarah and Punch walk back into the apartment.

EXT. BRUSSELS STREET 1—DAY

Sarah is walking Punch, looking at sights in Brussels.

EXT. BRUSSELS WARANDE PARK—DAY
*Sarah is jogging in the park, headphones on, with
Punch on a leash.*

EXT. BRUSSELS CAFE 1—EVENING
*Sarah is sitting outside at a cafe in Brussels, drinking
coffee, with Punch sitting next to her. She slips off her
shoes and tucks them under herself on the chair. Tom,
a tall, handsome young man walks by and doubletakes,
but keeps walking.*

CUT TO:
EXT. BRUSSELS CAFE 1—MOMENTS LATER
*Tom is walking past again with a drink in hand. He
stops, looks at something under the table, and
chuckles.*
TOM: Excuse me, miss. Do you like your shoes?
SARAH: *(Takes a second to look at Tom)* Uh. Don't you?
TOM: Well yes, but you might need a new pair now.
*Sarah looks for her shoes and sees Punch chewing
wildly on one of them.*
SARAH: Punch!
*Sarah tries to pull the shoe away and does not succeed.
Tom lifts a finger to indicate to Sarah that he will try to
help.*
*He crouches down, pats the dog on the head, holds his
hand out, and the dog drops the shoe in his hand
without hesitation.*
Tom sits at the table and gives her the shoe.

TOM: I know a good shoe repair shop.
Sarah Smiles.
Sarah and Tom are talking over a drink.
Tom takes the shoe and tries to stick the heel back on with chewing gum from his mouth. Sarah laughs at his effort.
Sarah and Tom are both leaning forward on the table and are flirting.
TOM (CONT'D): So you will come by tomorrow?
SARAH: *(Shrugs playfully)* Maybe.

INT. BRUSSELS MUSEUM—MORNING
Sarah is strolling around in a gallery looking at art. Tom approaches her.
TOM: Ready for your private tour Madame?
They kiss each other on the cheek.
Tom and Sarah are walking around, and Tom is showing Sarah some pieces explaining them.
Sarah is laughing about a particular piece.
Tom and Sarah are at the museum cafeteria drinking coffee and flirting.

INT. ELEVATOR MUSEUM—DAY
Tom and Sarah are kissing.

EXT. BRUSSELS MUSEUM—EVENING
Sarah and Tom walk out of the museum holding hands, exchanging glares and focussed on each other. The walk away from the museum together.

INT. TOM'S APARTMENT BEDROOM—EVENING
*A door is pushed open, and Sarah and Tom stumble
into the room while making out. Sarah pushes Tom
back for a second.*
SARAH: I have to go back home. I need to feed the dog.
*Tom leans in and kisses her again. Sarah kisses him
back passionately.*
SARAH: (CONT'D) *(leaning back for a second)* Alright,
but I'm not sleeping over.
FADE TO BLACK.

INT. TOM'S APARTMENT BEDROOM—MORNING
*Sarah slowly wakes up, covered with white sheets. Tom
stirs next to her. Sarah smiles to herself for a second
before jumping out in panic.*
SARAH: Punch!
INT. LAUREN'S APARTMENT ENTRANCE—MORNING
*A key is put into the door, and the door is opened.
Sarah walks into the apartment takes off her
headphones and takes Punch's leash off the shoe rack.
She looks into the apartment curiously.*
SARAH: Punch?
*When the dog doesn't come, Sarah walks further into
the apartment.*

INT. LAUREN'S APARTMENT LIVING-ROOM—
CONTINUOUS
Sarah finds Punch lying on the floor of the living room.

SARAH: Punch! *(cautiously walks over towards him)* Punch. Get up, boy. Let's go for a walk.

She approaches Punch and pokes him with a finger, but the dog doesn't move. Punch appears to be dead.

Sarah Looks around and finds a bottle of pills on the ground. The bottle has no label and is empty.

SARAH: (CONT'D) *(pacing the room, looking at the pill bottle)* Fuck, fuck, fuck, fuck, fuck,...

Finally, she stops pacing and looks at her phone on the table. She puts the pill bottle in her pocket and picks up the phone and dials.

SARAH: (CONT'D) Lauren. I'm so sorry.

(beat)

No, it's not a break in.

(beat)

No not a fire. Will you just let me talk? I killed your dog babe. I killed him. I'm so sorry. (beat)

Lauren? Lauren?

Sarah plops on the couch, thumbing her phone, unsure to call again.

Phone RINGS. Sarah picks up and listens. We hear the low murmur of Lauren talking.

SARAH: (CONT'D) I don't know. Please don't cry.

(beat)

I just came in, and he was....well.. (sobs)

I'm so sorry. I don't know what to do

(beat)

Yes, I'm sure he is dead!

(angrily) Who?

(beat)
The vet?
(beat)
But he is really dead.
(beat)
Oh. They do that. What, do you want him stuffed or something?
(We hear a sharp shout at the other end of phone)
Sorry. Course I'll call him.

CUT TO:
INT. LAUREN'S APARTMENT BEDROOM—LATER
Sarah is going through the drawer with the condoms, picks up a packet and stares at them woefully, then puts them back. She finds the dog's passport, with the vet's phone number in it. She sits on the edge of the bed and dials.

CUT TO:
INT. LAUREN'S APARTMENT BEDROOM—MOMENTS LATER
Sarah is pacing the room, head down, holding the phone to her ear.
SARAH: Is there any chance you could still do this today? The cost doesn't... (beat)
I see.
(beat)
What if I bring it, euh...him there?
FADE TO BLACK.

INT. LAUREN'S APARTMENT LIVING-ROOM—DAY
Sarah is walking around the apartment staring at Punch from every angle. She goes close to the animal and touches him, and tries to see if she can lift Punch to carry him, but it doesn't work out well practically. After taking a step back, she looks at the dog once more and looks like she has made a decision.

CUT TO:
INT. LAUREN'S APARTMENT LIVING-ROOM—MOMENTS LATER
Sarah puts down a suitcase next to the dog on the floor of the living room and opens it. She tries to lift the dog, with a clear expression of disgust on her face.

CUT TO:
INT. LAUREN'S BATHROOM—MOMENTS LATER
Sarah is bent over the toilet vomiting.

CUT TO:
INT. LAUREN'S APARTMENT LIVING-ROOM
Sarah picks up Punch, stuffs him in the suitcase and closes it up.

EXT. BRUSSELS STREET 1—AFTERNOON
Sarah has her headphones on and is dragging a suitcase in Brussels.

EXT. BRUSSELS WARANDE PARK—AFTERNOON
Sarah, still wearing her headphones, is dragging the suitcase through the park. She accidentally lets go of the handle and the suitcase slams to the ground. We hear a WHINE once or twice. Sarah picks the handle back up and continues walking.

INT. BRUSSELS METRO STATION 1—AFTERNOON
Sarah is struggling with dragging a suitcase up the stairs in a Brussels metro station, as a tall and lanky YOUNG MAN, wearing a training suit and red sneakers, notices her. He walks over to her while she is at the lower part of the stairs.
YOUNG MAN: *(Gesturing towards the suitcase)*
Je peux vous aider?
SARAH: Nono,...
YOUNG MAN: Venez. Je t'aiderai!
SARAH: (reluctantly)
Eh, ok, yes thank you.
The young man nods and picks up the suitcase. They start walking up the stairs.
YOUNG MAN: You live in Brussels?
SARAH: Ah, no, I'm just visiting a friend for a few days.
YOUNG MAN: Heavy bag. What did you bring?
SARAH: Oh just some computer parts. I work in IT.

O.S. The metro SCREECHES as it comes pulling into the station.
The young man smiles and nods a few times. He pauses

to put the suitcase down for a second and stretches his back. He lifts the suitcase and suddenly starts running up and away with it.
Sarah is standing there looking shocked, for a split second, before she reacts and shouts after him.

O.S. The metro doors BEEP to signal they are closing.
He is already at the top of the stairs. Sarah starts running up and reaches the platform just in time to see the metro leave with the young man in it. She stands there looking around for a moment, before she walks back down the stairs.

INT. BRUSSELS NORTH TRAIN STATION—EARLY EVENING
The young man walks up the stairs carrying the suitcase and walks to a corner of the station. He puts the suitcase against a wall and looks around him with a smile.
He put the suitcase down to open it. Suddenly there is some movement in the suitcase. The young man is surprised, yet cautiously he opens the suitcase.
YOUNG MAN: *(looking inside the suitcase)* Oh, *putain*!
Punch gets up and growls at him baring his teeth. The young man is paralyzed with shock.
YOUNG MAN (CONT'D) Shhhhhhh...
Punch jumps up at him.
FADE TO BLACK.

EXT. BRUSSELS CAFE 1—DAY

Lauren and Sarah are sitting outside the cafe having a drink. People with dogs keep passing them by. Lauren suddenly lets out a sob.

SARAH: I can't tell you how sorry I am.

LAUREN: I just don't get it. There was nothing wrong with Punch. What did the vet say?

SARAH: He said he died in his sleep. I'm sorr...

LAUREN: Thanks for finding that other vet at the last minutes.

BARKING in the background.

Tom is walking by and stops suddenly when he sees Sarah.

TOM: Hey! Sarah! How are you?

Tom suddenly stops in his tracks and looks at Lauren in shock.

LAUREN: Tom? Hey!

TOM: Hey babe. I thought you were coming back on Friday.

LAUREN: I was.

(Hesitating)

How do you know Sarah?

SARAH: *(mumbling)* Lauren, I ...

Sarah suddenly stops and gets up from her seat. From behind Lauren, Punch walks up, a red sneaker in his mouth, and sits down next to her dropping the sneaker in front of him. Lauren screams and jumps off her seat, and Punch sits up and barks back at her. Lauren throws

Sarah a look of shock. Tom looks at the dog and back at Sarah. Sarah just keeps staring at the dog in disbelief.

*

Hamed Mobasser *is an aspiring scriptwriter and filmmaker in Brussels. In the past two years, he has been co-writing feature-length screenplays and series with the collective Punchdog Productions (www.facebook.com/punchdogproductions), one of which, entitled Luna, was shortlisted in the Geronimo productions short film script competition, 2016. He is working on two comedy scripts and a drama series to be pitched in 2018.*

Kevin Dwyer

Little Piggy Come to Play

This is the first chapter of a novel-in-progress tentatively entitled Bodily States. The novel traces the tortuous relationship of a brother and sister—Ted and Amber—as they evolve from childhood to adulthood in an increasingly dystopic society in which fat and obesity become taboo and then outlawed. While Amber easily adapts to the fat reforms and becomes a fit and firm member of society, her attempts to help Ted control his appetite and body mass all fail, and Ted will be banished to the Fatlands. In the end, both find spiritual grace, Amber as an ordained "fasting woman," and Ted as an overfed object of worship.

FRIDAY HAD ARRIVED, and Ted and Amber palpitated as one with excitement. Mom and Dad announced earlier in the week that they were invited to a dinner party and that the kids would be home alone on Friday evening, with no babysitter, under Amber's supervision. For the first time Mom and Dad were trusting Amber to take care of Ted. It was to be her first real performance as big sister. Diabolical plans for fun immediately surfaced in her mind. Tonight there would be no adult around to tell them what they could and couldn't do. The house would be their playground. There wasn't just the TV, the computer and video games, but there were plenty of forbidden corners of the house that needed exploring, especially in their parents' bedroom. Mom left very solemn and precise instructions. Ted was on a strict timeline for the evening, but Amber knew there was not the slimmest chance she would stick to it. She had other plans for Ted. They would play a big game. She would be Q, and he would be James Bond. With promises of goodies from Dad's "treasure chest", it would be easy to convince her roly-poly little brother to be her master spy, and she would send him snooping into the furthest reaches of the house in search of secrets and lies. Amber was certain they lay hidden somewhere between the bedroom and the kitchen.

It was an important night for Dad as well. Some friends were celebrating an anniversary with a party. Mom and Dad had not been getting along well. There were hushed arguments late in the night. As far as Amber could tell, it was always about money and bills, especially the expensive stuff Dad kept buying. Dad wanted to leave his job as the breakfast chef at Wilmot's Diner and open his own restaurant. It was a bad time for restaurants, there was a big slump all-around since the Taco Bell case, and the trans-fat regulations were passed. On the positive side, this had brought prices down, and Dad had his eyes on a good deal for a place in Fresno. It was a dream of Dad's. He was always testing new dishes at home, preparing his ideal menu, going through catalogues and selecting equipment for his fantasy kitchen. There was spreadsheet upon spreadsheet, but none of the calculations worked out. There was no profit to be found in the restaurant business anymore. So many were closing down.

There would be friends of friends at the party tonight who, Dad was told, might consider financing his restaurant. Peter had minutely prepared an assortment of dishes for them to sample as a sort of hors-d'oeuvre. He called them mini-tapas, which Mom said was ridiculous because tapas were already very mini. He thought of bringing the wines that matched each dish, but Janice was dead against the idea. It was not a pot luck, and Janice thought Peter was overdoing it, acting desperate and needy. But then again, Mom and Dad disagreed on almost everything lately.

Mom was convinced that Dad's dream would lead the family into financial ruin and opposed it ferociously at every turn of the road. Their arguments became strident. Some nights Dad stormed out and slept on the couch, snoring away without a care in the world. On other nights Amber heard her mother getting up when all was dark, weeping her way to the kitchen. Amber spied on her from the top of the stairs as she removed packages and jars from the fridge and cupboards and started to eat, and eat, and eat, standing up at the counter. Just when Amber thought she was done eating Mom would take ice cream from the freezer compartment and go at the carton directly with a big spoon. As she scooped the ice cream into her mouth, tears would stream down her cheeks, but she never stopped until the carton was finished, dumping it afterwards into the trash along with the spoon. Amber couldn't understand. If Mom liked eating so much, why was she crying?

For Ted and Amber's supper on Friday, Mom left out a casserole to warm up of macaroni and cheese that she prepared from the blue and yellow package. It only needed to be microwaved. That would be a job for Ted. Amber didn't go near the microwave. She had written a report about those waves for school and knew what they were capable of, how they could penetrate everything everywhere and start cancers and cause birth defects. Mom and Dad were perplexed at Amber's adamancy and thought it a teenage quirk. She held her belly and left the room whenever the microwave was running, and couldn't stand the smell of it, every time that little oven door was opened, it stank up the whole house. Even up in her room with the door closed, she knew when someone left the microwave open. Mom also set out a package of cookies for them to share after dinner, and then there was a bag of popcorn for watching TV. Ted was to be in bed by 10 o'clock, a stretch of the usual rules, but tonight was an exception, so he could stay up longer. Ted knew from experience that the best way to get the cookies was to eat the macaroni and cheese first, so the minute the car pulled out of the garage and drove off, he programmed the microwave and slipped in the casserole, dreamily watching it rotate and bubble in the light of the oven. Amber took her distance across the room.

"I wouldn't put my head near that thing while it's on."

"Why not?"

"They don't know half of what they should about those waves. If they can go in your food, they can go in your brain." Amber returned from the far side of the room after the bell rang. Not happy with the level of sizzling Ted pushed the button again. Amber opened the package of cookies and started to eat one.

"Hey! You can't Am, you have to eat dinner first! Mom said we have to share."

"Where's Mom now?"

Parents were unfair and cruel all the time, and now it was her chance. Amber held up a cookie. "This is my dinner. Mom left me in charge. You, on the other hand, have to finish all your macaroni and cheese, or no cookies." The oven bell rang, and Amber plopped the sizzling fluorescent cheesy dish in front of Ted. "Go on now, Mom made it 'cause it's your favorite."

Ted forked the dripping, creamy orange tubes into his mouth. As Ted ate, Amber held a cookie and waved it in the air around her, watching Ted's hungry gaze follow the cookie's peregrinations. Amber marveled at the force behind food, and the even greater force that cookies seemed to wield. Ted gorged his body while his mind thought only of what he would eat next. They were all alike in that way, Ted, Mom and Dad, held in food's sway, living lives punctuated by three meals a day, with nibbles and bites, snacks and appetizers in between. Nothing but food. Amber watched her brother chew like a mindless cow, so unaware of what was taking place in his mouth. There was a new nutrition class at school, part of the curriculum changes being phased in. They did an experiment in class where they had to collect their own saliva (by spitting for a week in a jar!) and then spread it over different foods. Amber looked at the perpetual motion of Ted's mouth, opening, chewing, swallowing, and imagined his enzyme-packed mouth juices rolling off his tongue and down the walls of his mouth, mixing with the chemicals in the cheese powder. If it was just to become a useless lump like her brother, what was the point of eating at all? Sure he was happy but how long would it last? The other kids were already making fun of him at school.

"I'm done. Time for a cookie!" Ted slid his dish away from him, but there was still a spoonful of noodles in the casserole. In loco parentis, Amber shook her head.

"No, you're not. Clean your plate."

"Come on, Am."

"Just a few more bites. If you can eat cookies, you

can finish what's left on your dish first. And then we'll play James Bond."

Ted never knew where Amber got the notion that he liked playing James Bond with her. It was her idea, her game. As James Bond, he had to do whatever she, as Q, requested and he would get rewards afterwards. Sometimes she would make him do funny things, and he made her laugh with that cruel accent, but in the end she always bossed him around too much, and they fought. Sometimes Dad would join in too when he was around. He would always play the Evil One and sit on the couch and cackle pretending to stroke his big white cat.

"Mr Bond, your first assignment is quite simple. Go to the cupboard and bring me three of the magic treasure bags where the Evil One gets his powers."

"Amber, you know we can't go in there. Dad said."

"You know the rules, Mister Bond. Do it for Her Majesty."

Ted disappeared into the living room while Amber cleared the dishes. He came back with three aluminum bags ruffling in his pudgy arms. Amber took the bounty and admired it: Cheezy Chips, Tortilla Pops, and Pork Rindz.

"You have exceeded our expectations, Mister Bond. We are all pleased with your work. Please accept your reward."

Amber placed the three bags on the table and presented Ted with two cookies. While Ted gratefully munched away, Amber inspected the booty, holding each of the bags to the light and taking note. She was just learning to read the nutritional information on food packages at school. She saw that the Pork Rindz easily had the highest calorie content and put them aside for later.

"Very good indeed. This gives the Evil One so much of his strength and power. You do want to take it all away from him and be just as big and powerful, don't you?"

"Yes, Ma'am. For the Crown."

Amber opened the bag of Cheezy Chips and held one by the tips of her fingers before Ted's mouth as if delivering the Eucharist.

"For the Crown."

Ted nodded, opened his mouth and received the chip on his tongue. The ritual was repeated twice before Amber took charge again. She sent Ted on other missions in the bedroom, in the garage and in the bathroom, while she went through the far reaches of the kitchen cupboards, taking note of all the contents. Dad had amassed a collection of brightly-labelled, foreign-looking cans and jars. Amber recognized French and Spanish and Italian on some of the labels, but there were also other languages and alphabets that she could not decipher at all. The price tags showed that Dad was paying a lot for all this food from far away. She opened one of the jars with French writing that said *rillettes* and then *pur porc*. She saw nothing but a layer of thick white fat. She poked a knife in the jar and under the fat was a something grey and meaty, but the acrid pet food smell made her nose crinkle and stomach turn. She closed the jar before any more of that smell could escape in the air around her and returned it to the cupboard. Is this what Dad was spending a fortune on? She remembered Mom's vows and all the arguments against the restaurant. While Amber was lost in the discovery of the pantry Ted was finishing the cookies. He stopped in mid-chew and smiled at his sister. His cheeks were bright red, and beads of sweat gathered above his lip.

"Your next mission is a sensitive one, Mister Bond. Should you decide to accept it, you are to go to the nether chamber of the Evil One and bring back anything that does not belong to him, for he has stolen it and it must be returned to its rightful owner. Her Majesty will reward you generously if you succeed."

"You want me to spy around in the cellar?"

Amber shook the bag of Pork Rindz at Ted.

"Do as Her Majesty commands. Yours is not to reason why. Find the secrets before the Evil One returns to his lair, Mr Bond."

Ted walked heavily downstairs. Amber folded her legs on the couch. She reached for the empty foil wrapper of the Cheezy Chips and ran her fingertip along the greasy inside of the package. She rubbed the dusty remains of the savory flavoring into her gums. She was not like them. She was well aware that all that she ate she became her. She was comforted by the way her skin wrapped so nicely around her bones. Feeling intact was the most important sensation for her, and she knew it was a feeling she would keep the rest of her life. It was hers and hers alone, something she could keep and have. It helped her pull in the reins when things started to get out of control. Ted came up the stairs some ten minutes later. Amber never liked it down in the cellar and preferred to keep all of her business above ground. Ted appeared before her as a miniature version of Dad. His belly was taking on the same lumpy form. His thighs rubbed together in the same repulsive way. He held something behind his back.

"What have you found, Mr Bond? Show me."

Ted shook his head, but he burst out snickering. It was too weird, but it was funny. He slowly moved his arms around. First, in one hand there was a book, the latest diet book Mom was secretly reading as she sat by the washing machine. In the other, he dangled a leather dog collar with a long, felt leash. Ted read the writing on the collar.

"It says... Brownie. Is it a dog collar? Is it for a surprise? Is this the secret?"

*

Ted was too young to remember. Brownie was a cocker spaniel puppy Mom and Dad bought a long time ago for Amber's 7th birthday. At six weeks Brownie had the sweetest of chirpy little barks and loved to lick Amber's face. The more she giggled, the more Brownie licked until it became unbearable for her. One day they were all out for a walk, Ted was still in his stroller. Brownie wore his brand-new collar and was on the leash. They took turns running around in circles with the puppy who never tired of the fun, held aloft by his long floppy ears. Dad was holding the leash with Brownie running at his side. Dad cut to the left then to the right then to the left again. Brownie couldn't keep up with all the turns and ran to the right as Dad's heavy booted foot headed to the left and stepped right on him. Brownie didn't move, save for the final heaving breaths he took and the blood trickling through his nostrils. The crushed puppy lay still, and they all stared down in shock and dismay. Amber rubbed Brownie's forehead and said his name softly, but she knew there was nothing to be done. Dad was sheepish and apologetic, but there was nothing of the sheep about him. He was a fat pig of a monster who just crushed a defenseless puppy. Amber's gaze rose from the deadly tread marks of Dad's boot to the pudgy calves and cellulite thighs, to the broad belly, to the drooping jowls, bleating and blathering pathetic penance. 258 pounds against 3. Brownie had no chance.

"Give it here. Is this all you could find, Mr Bond? Her Majesty will be very disappointed."

Amber accepted the collar and held it in her palms. Dad said it was an accident, that there was nothing he could do, that these things happen. Weighing 258 pounds is not an accident, it's not something that just happens. Brownie had no chance.

"This will not do. For your next mission Mister Bond, you will have to go under cover. As a dog. Put it on." Amber held out the leash. "Go on. This is very delicate, but if you want to serve the Crown, you have to put this on and get on all fours. Now, doggy, do it. In fact, you'll have a new undercover name. I'll call you Doggy. Okay, Doggy?"

The game had a logic that had to be followed. Ted could only be rewarded for surpassing his previous tasks. Amber led Ted around the living room floor on the leash, pulling him harder when he lagged behind. She stopped every now and then to pet him on the head and feed him from one of the bags of snacks she carried. Ted rolled on the floor as commanded. His t-shirt slid up on him and revealed his mountainous midriff. Amber tugged at Brownie's collar and led Ted barking to the kitchen. The collar barely fit around his neck. Fat little boys, daddies and sons, deserved nothing more.

"You're such a fat little doggy, aren't you? And you do eat so much. I think I'll call you little piggy now. Do you like being called little piggy? Can you do little piggy tricks for me? Can you oink for me? Oink oink. Now roll over for me and show me your belly. Look here there's even some pork rinds. You're such a little piggy that you'd even eat the fat skin of other little piggies, wouldn't you? That's a good little piggy. Would you like ketchup on them?"

Amber turned to the counter and squeezed the thick red sauce over the pork rind. She fed it right into her brother's open mouth. Ted screamed first from surprise then from the intense burning sensation. Amber held up one of Dad's expensive bottles that said Real West Indian Scotch Bonnet Pepper Sauce. They all cried when they ate in the end. Amber filled a bowl with root beer and placed it on the floor.

"Whoops, sorry little piggy, I mistook the ketchup for hot sauce. Aww, now don't feel so bad. Go drink from your bowl; it will make your big old belly feel better. Go on, lap up that sweet, sweet drink. That's it; there's more where that came from."

*

Mom and Dad stood on the threshold of the kitchen. Ted was on all fours on the floor wearing a dog leash— Brownie's leash—held by Amber standing before him with her slippered foot on his shoulder. Ted was red-faced, Amber was forcing him down to the ground beside a heap of debris that had been dumped from the trash basket. In her other hand, Amber held a jar of Peter's finest French *rillettes* with a spoon sticking trying to feed it to Ted. Amber turned toward her parents. They all stared at each other in dumbstruck awe.

"Mom, Dad. We were just playing. You know, having a little fun. Ted... wanted to be a dog... but he ended up being a pig. Didn't you Ted?"

*

Kevin Dwyer *has been writing short stories, novels and film scripts for over thirty years, lately as a member of Punchdog Productions. His short story 'Candy' was adapted into the short film O-Zone in 2003, and his script* Doing It for Marilyn *is currently being made into a short film, directed by Kevork Aslanyan.*

More books from
Harvard Square Editions

Reader, we would love to hear your thoughts on The Circle. *If you enjoyed this book, please leave a review!*

www.ingramcontent.com/pod-product-compliance
Lightning Source LLC
Chambersburg PA
CBHW020529020726
47494CB00006B/1690